16 EXTRAORDINARY
ASIAN
AMERICANS

NANCY LOBB

J. WESTON
WALCH
PUBLISHER
Portland, Maine

Photo Credits

Daniel K. Inouye	Photo courtesy of United States Senate
Maxine Hong Kingston	Photo © Jerry Bauer, Alfred A. Knopf
I.M. Pei	© 1988 AP/WIDE WORLD PHOTOS
Maya Lin	Photo by Michael Marsland Courtesy of Yale University Office of Public Affairs
An Wang	© 1988 UPI/CORBIS-BETTMAN
Haing Ngor	© 1985 P.H. Zanger UPI/BETTMAN
Seiji Ozawa	© 1986 Tsugufami Matsumoto AP/WIDE WORLD PHOTOS
Kristi Yamaguchi	© 1992 John Gaps III AP/WIDE WORLD PHOTOS
Noriyuki "Pat" Morita	© AP/WIDE WORLD PHOTOS
Yo-Yo Ma	© 1985 Michael Lutch, WGBH Educational Foundation AP/WIDE WORLD PHOTOS
David Ho	Photo courtesy of The Aaron Diamond AIDS Research Center for the City of New York
Wendy Lee Gramm	© 1989 Rick Bowme AP/WIDE WORLD PHOTOS
Ellison Onizuka	Photo courtesy of NASA
Carlos Bulosan	Photo by Francisco Belandres AP/WIDE WORLD PHOTOS
Jose Aruego	Photo courtesy of Simon & Schuster, Children's Publishing Division
Dustin Nguyen	© Albert Chacon/Shooting Star

1   2   3   4   5   6   7   8   9   10

ISBN 0-8251-2858-7

Copyright © 1996
J. Weston Walch, Publisher
P. O. Box 658 • Portland, Maine 04104-0658

Printed in the United States of America

Contents

Introduction

The lives of many Asian Americans have made a difference in the story of America. Writers, artists, scientists, teachers, politicians, ministers, lawyers, doctors, businesspeople, athletes, and so many more have helped to make America what it is today. Asian Americans can be proud of their heritage. It is a pride all Americans can share.

In this book, you will read the stories of 16 of these people:

- Daniel K. Inouye, United States Senator from Hawaii, who was the first Japanese American to be elected to Congress

- Maxine Hong Kingston, an author whose acclaimed books tell of Chinese-American contributions to American society

- I.M. Pei, one of the world's leading architects

- Maya Lin, a sculptor who is best known for designing the Vietnam Veterans Memorial in Washington, D.C.

- An Wang, scientist, inventor, and founder of Wang Laboratories

- Haing Ngor, a physician who won an Academy Award for his first movie role, playing Dith Pran in *The Killing Fields*

- Seiji Ozawa, conductor of the Boston Symphony Orchestra for over 20 years

- Kristi Yamaguchi, winner of an Olympic gold medal in women's figure skating in the 1992 Olympic Games

- Noriyuki "Pat" Morita, an actor whose best-known role was the karate master Miyagi in *The Karate Kid* series

- Yo-Yo Ma, the finest cellist in the world today

- David Ho, physician and medical researcher who has made important discoveries in the fight against AIDS

- Wendy Lee Gramm, an economist who was chair of the Commodities Futures Trading Commission

- Ellison Onizuka, an astronaut who lost his life in the explosion of the *Challenger* space shuttle in 1986

- Carlos Bulosan, a poet and writer whose book *America Is in the Heart* became a classic in Asian-American literature

- Jose Aruego, an illustrator of children's books

- Dustin Nguyen, an actor who works against drugs and gangs

People have come to the United States from Asian countries for many years. These Asian countries include Japan, China, Taiwan, Vietnam, Cambodia, Korea, the Philippines, the Pacific Islands, and many others.

In the 1800's, Asians came to the United States in search of economic opportunity. They came to work in the sugarcane fields of Hawaii. They worked in the California Gold Rush. Others helped build the transcontinental railroad.

More recently, many Asians have come to America to escape war in their native lands. Many refugees have arrived from Cambodia, Laos, and Vietnam.

The 1990 Census showed 7,273,662 Asian Americans in the United States. That is about 3 percent of the total United States population.

Most Asian Americans live in Hawaii, making up 62 percent of the population in that state. Other states with many Asian

Americans are California, Oregon, Washington, New York, Alabama, and New Jersey.

Asian Americans tend to be disciplined, hardworking people. They are high achievers who are making significant contributions to American society.

The motto on the Great Seal of the United States reads "E PLURIBUS UNUM." That is Latin for "Out of Many, One." The United States is made up of many peoples who have come together to form one nation. Each group has been an important part of American history. I hope you will enjoy reading about 16 Asian Americans who have made a difference.

—Nancy Lobb

Daniel K. Inouye

United States Senator

"Mama," the little boy asked, "could a poor boy like me grow up to marry the daughter of the emperor of Japan?"

"Son," his mother answered, "remember always that there is no one who is too good for you. But remember, too, that you are no better than anyone else, either."

Daniel Ken Inouye never forgot his mother's words. He grew up and became a United States senator from Hawaii. He has earned the respect of his fellow senators and of the American public. He has always worked for the rights of all people.

Inouye was born in 1924 in Honolulu, Hawaii. He was the oldest of four children. His father had come to Hawaii from Japan as a child. That made the Inouye children "nisei." Nisei means the children were born in America to parents who came to America from Japan.

Inouye's father worked as a file clerk to support his family. The family was poor. They lived in the Japanese ghetto in Honolulu.

To save money, Inouye's mother bought his shoes two sizes too big. Then she stuffed them with paper to make them fit. This never bothered Inouye, as he preferred to go barefoot.

Inouye grew up learning both Japanese and American customs. He learned to speak Japanese before he spoke English. He went to public school. Then, after public school, he went to a Japanese school for two hours a day. There he learned to read and write in Japanese. He also learned Japanese history and customs.

In Hawaii, most nisei children learned English as a second language. Most of their families spoke a mixture of English, Japanese, Chinese, and Hawaiian known as "pidgin." Since they rarely heard standard English spoken, very few nisei children could speak standard English.

So the whites in Hawaii thought of a plan to keep the nisei children out of "white schools." At age 12, all children who spoke English as a second language had to take the English Standard test. Those who passed were admitted to English Standard schools. These schools had the best buildings and teachers.

It was rare for nisei to pass the test. Inouye did not pass. He went on to McKinley High, also known as "Tokyo High." But he had big plans for himself. He wanted to become a surgeon. He studied books on medicine. He took the Red Cross course in first aid. He began teaching first aid to others.

When Inouye was a senior in high school, disaster struck. On December 7, 1941, the Japanese bombed the U.S. Navy base at Pearl Harbor, Hawaii. Thousands of people were killed or wounded. Most of the ships in Pearl Harbor were destroyed or badly damaged. The United States was thrown into World War II.

Dan Inouye was ordered to report to the Red Cross station to help give first aid to the many wounded. For a week, he worked day and night. After that, he slowed down to a 12-hour shift: 6 P.M. to 6 A.M. At the same time, he finished his senior year in high school.

Japanese Americans were ashamed of Japan's actions. They were loyal Americans. But many white Americans did not trust

Japanese Americans. They were afraid some might prove to be spies. So for the first year of the war no nisei were allowed to join the armed forces.

Inouye enrolled in the premedical program at the University of Hawaii. And he continued working at the Red Cross station.

Young Japanese Americans asked Congress to allow them to prove their loyalty by fighting in the army. Finally, the rule was changed. The 442nd Infantry Regimental Combat Team became the first all-volunteer and first all-nisei combat team. Inouye dropped out of college to sign up.

The 442nd was nicknamed the "Go for Broke" combat team. That meant the men would give it everything they had. It became the most decorated army unit in U.S. history. The story of the 442nd Combat Team is told in the 1951 MGM movie *Go for Broke!*

Just two days before the war in Europe ended, 2nd Lieutenant Inouye led a charge on a heavily defended German-held hill. He was shot in the stomach and legs. His right arm was shattered by a rifle grenade. Yet he went on, throwing grenades into three enemy machine-gun nests. Inouye's actions saved his unit from certain destruction.

For his bravery, Inouye was awarded the Distinguished Service Cross, along with a number of other honors. But Inouye spent the next two years in army hospitals recovering from his wounds. His arm could not be saved.

Inouye was discharged from the army as a captain. He returned to Hawaii in 1947. But Inouye knew he could no longer become a surgeon. So he changed to the study of law, with the idea of going into politics.

Inouye graduated from college in 1950. He went on to George Washington University Law School, graduating in 1952.

Returning to Hawaii, Inouye entered politics. At that time, Hawaii was not yet a state. It was an American territory. That meant that Hawaiians were U.S. citizens. They could send representatives to Congress. But those representatives did not have a vote.

The Republican party controlled the Hawaiian legislature. But Inouye joined the Democratic party. He hoped the Democrats would work to give Asian Americans more rights.

In 1954, Inouye was elected to the territorial House of Representatives. He became the majority leader at age 30. Four years later, he was elected to the territorial Senate.

In 1959, Hawaii became our fiftieth state. Inouye was elected to Hawaii's first seat in the U.S. House of Representatives. He was the first Japanese American to be elected to Congress.

In 1962, Inouye was elected to the U.S. Senate. He has been reelected to this job ever since.

Inouye made his mark quickly as a strong supporter of the civil rights movement of the 1960's. He knew firsthand what discrimination was all about.

Inouye became known as a skillful negotiator and leader. In 1973, he was appointed to the Senate Watergate Committee. This committee had to find out if crimes had been committed during President Nixon's 1972 reelection campaign. The Watergate hearings were on national television for weeks. Inouye gained respect for his patient, skillful questioning of witnesses during these hearings. (The hearings led Nixon to resign in 1974.)

In 1974, a number of illegal activities by the CIA and FBI came to light. The Senate set up a Select Committee on Intelligence in 1976 to oversee these agencies. Inouye was chosen as the chairman for this committee.

In 1987, he was chosen to lead the Iran-Contra hearings. This committee investigated secret sales of weapons by the U.S. government to Iran. It investigated the use of the profits from those sales to help the Contras in Nicaragua overthrow their government.

Inouye serves on a number of important Senate committees. Currently as chairman of the Appropriations Committee's subcommittee on foreign operations, he oversees foreign aid.

Inouye is married and has one son. He has homes in Washington, D.C., and Honolulu. His office is decorated with Hawaiian crafts, tropical fish tanks, and tropical plants.

Inouye has been in the U.S. Congress since 1959. He has won the admiration of his fellow congressmen for his ability to work out compromises. He is known for his integrity and honesty.

Remembering the Facts

1. What does the word *nisei* mean?

2. How were the nisei children segregated from whites in Hawaii?

3. How did Inouye work toward his goal of becoming a surgeon?

4. What happened on December 7, 1941?

5. Name two unique things about the 442nd Infantry Regimental Combat Team in World War II.

6. Why did Inouye give up the study of medicine for law?

7. What two "firsts" did Inouye become in 1959?

8. During what two famous televised hearings did Inouye win the admiration of the American people?

Understanding the Story

9. Why do you think white Americans were so afraid of their Japanese-American neighbors during World War II? Do you think there were any ways this fear could have been avoided?

10. Why do you think it was so difficult for nisei children to learn to speak standard English?

Getting the Main Idea

Why do you think the story of Daniel Inouye is an important part of American history?

Applying What You've Learned

What message do you think Daniel Inouye brings to any group of minorities?

Maxine Hong Kingston

Author

Maxine Hong Kingston is a Chinese-American writer. Her books tell the story of Chinese-American contributions in American history.

Kingston was born in 1940 in Stockton, California. She was the first of six children.

Her father was born in China. He was trained from birth to be a scholar. After passing his exams, he became a teacher in the village of Sun Woi. He did not enjoy teaching. In 1924 he decided to leave China for a better life.

Upon arriving in New York City, he changed his name to Tom, after

Maxine Hong Kingston

Thomas Edison. He was unable to find work as a teacher or poet. So, he found a job in a laundry. For the next 15 years, he sent money to his wife, Ying Lan, who had remained behind in China.

Ying Lan Hong was not idle while she waited for her husband to send for her. For two years, she went to school to learn medicine and midwifery. She then returned to Sun Woi to practice medicine. Refusing to treat those who were obviously dying, she became known as a very successful healer.

By 1939, Tom Hong had saved enough money to send for his wife. The couple moved to Stockton, California. There Tom ran a gambling house. When Maxine was born, she was named after a blond gambler who was very lucky.

Later, the Hongs bought a laundry. They named it Stockton's New Port Laundry. All six children worked long hours in the laundry. In fact, the family spent more hours there than they did at home. The laundry became a gathering place for the Chinese people living in Stockton.

It was at the laundry that Maxine heard stories of her Chinese culture. The Chinese spoke in "talk stories." This form of storytelling mixed family stories with the myths, legends, and history of China. Ying Lan Hong was a gifted storyteller. Her "talk stories" gave her daughter the material she used later in writing her books.

As a child, Maxine spoke a form of Cantonese. No English was spoken in her home. When she began grade school, she was very shy and refused to speak at all.

She was not a model student. She covered all her drawings with black paint. She scribbled with chalk over her board work. Her teachers did not know what to do with her. Her parents could not talk to her teachers, since they did not speak English. Only she knew that she was covering her work with a black "stage curtain." Under the curtain were her surprises just waiting to be uncovered.

Her parents were very unhappy with her poor work in school. Finally, they reminded her that in China parents and teachers of criminals were put to death. That scared her into trying harder in school. As she grew older, she began getting straight *A*'s.

After regular school, she went to Chinese school from 5:00 to 7:00 P.M. There the students were taught Chinese history and culture. In Chinese school, she felt free to let loose and act more like a normal child.

By the age of nine, she had learned much English. She began writing poems and stories. It soon became clear that she had her mother's gift for storytelling. At the age of 15, Maxine published her first work. It was an essay about growing up as a Chinese American. For her work, she was paid $5 by *Girl Scout Magazine.*

After high school, she went to the University of California at Berkeley. She won 11 scholarships, one after another. Since she was good in math, she studied engineering. Soon she switched to English literature.

At this time, she met her future husband, Earll Kingston. They were married in 1962.

Berkeley during the 1960's was a hotbed of student unrest. Students were protesting the Vietnam War. The values of the older generation were in question. It was the time of the hippies, who hoped to change the world for the better.

The Kingstons were well matched. Both marched against the Vietnam War. Both became ministers of the Universal Life Church. And both loved the theater. The next year their son, Joseph, was born.

Kingston hoped to become a writer. But she realized that most writers can't make a living. So she went back to school to get a teaching certificate.

In the late 1960's, the family moved to Hawaii. For the next 10 years, Kingston taught in several schools.

In 1976, she published her first book. *The Woman Warrior: Memoirs of a Girlhood Among Ghosts* tells of her childhood as a Chinese-American girl.

The woman warrior of the title uses a sword to fight for the rights of the oppressed. In China, women and girls were second-class citizens. Young girls were bought and sold like slaves. Chinese girls grew up hearing old sayings like "Better to raise geese than girls."

The ghosts in the title are the white people of Stockton. They are also the spirits of her Chinese ancestors. Young Maxine had been confused and pulled in different ways by her two cultures.

The Woman Warrior became a best-seller. It also won the National Book Critics Circle Award as the best nonfiction book of the year. Kingston was on her way.

In 1980, Kingston published her second book: *China Men.* This book tells the story of the men in her family. They labored in steaming laundries. They cleared the land for the Hawaiian sugar fields. They helped build the transcontinental railroad. Chinese men helped to build America. By doing so, they earned the right to be seen as citizens with full rights.

Kingston's third book was *Tripmaster Monkey: His Fake Book.* It was published in 1989. It tells the story of a Berkeley graduate during the time of the Vietnam War.

Kingston has written many short stories, poems, and articles. She no longer has to teach to support herself. But she does work-shops and guest lectures from time to time.

In 1980, Kingston won a very special award. She was named a "Living Treasure of Hawaii." She was the first Chinese American to win this award, usually given to someone over 80. She has won many other awards over the years.

Kingston grew up during a time when women, especially Chinese women, had no rights and no voice. But Kingston found her voice as a writer. She came to realize that as a writer she had a power as great as the Woman Warrior's sword. She could use her words to help change things that were wrong.

She writes too about the right the Chinese Americans have earned to full status as Americans. Their contributions to American life have been great. She says, "What I am doing . . . is claiming America." She writes about becoming American "in spite of rejection and misunderstanding."

Kingston has made an outstanding contribution to the under-standing and acceptance of one group of Americans, the Chinese Americans.

Remembering the Facts

1. Why did Tom Hong take a job in a laundry?

2. How long did Ying Lan Hong wait in China for her husband to send for her?

3. What did Ying Lan do while she waited for her husband?

4. How did Maxine get her name?

5. What is a "talk story"?

6. Where did Kingston gather the material for her books?

7. Why did she have trouble when she started school?

8. What is *The Woman Warrior* about?

9. What is the subject of *China Men*, her second book?

Understanding the Story

10. In China, women and girls were seen as little better than slaves. What effect do you think sayings like "Better to raise geese than girls" would have on a young girl?

11. Writers often speak out against the wrongs they see around them. What wrongs did Kingston write about?

Getting the Main Idea

What do you think is the most important contribution Maxine Hong Kingston has made toward the acceptance of Chinese Americans into American culture?

Applying What You've Learned

Write a poem or short story in which you tell about part of your own background. Use family stories, local myths, or legends woven together in the style of a Chinese "talk story."

I.M. Pei

Architect

- John F. Kennedy Library, Boston, Massachusetts

- National Center for Atmospheric Research, Boulder, Colorado

- Bank of China, Hong Kong

- Louvre addition, Paris, France

- Rock 'n' Roll Hall of Fame, Cleveland, Ohio

I.M. Pei

What do all these buildings (and many more) have in common? All were designed by one of the most famous architects of today, I.M. Pei.

Pei was born in 1917 in Canton, China. His full name is Ieoh Ming Pei. That means "to inscribe brightly."

Pei was the oldest son of five children of a wealthy banker. When he was just a year old, his family moved to Hong Kong, a British colony. There, he learned to speak English.

When Pei was nine years old, the family moved to Shanghai. It was a booming city with many new buildings going up. Pei was especially fascinated with a 23-story skyscraper. His interest in architecture became intense.

Pei was very close to his mother. She was a gifted musician and a devout Buddhist. Young Pei went with her on retreats to Buddhist temples. When he was only 13, his mother died.

Pei's father hoped his son would become a doctor. But young Pei had no interest in medicine. His love was architecture and building.

In those days, well-to-do Chinese often sent their children abroad to study. So, it was not unusual that Pei decided he wanted to study architecture in America. In 1935, at the age of 17, he sailed off to the United States. His plan was to complete his studies there and then return to China.

Pei began his studies at the University of Pennsylvania. He did not enjoy the program there. There was too much study of drawing for his liking. So he transferred to Massachusetts Institute of Technology to study engineering. He got his degree in 1940.

Pei was ready to return to China. But his plans did not work out. Japan had invaded China, and war was going on. Then in 1941, the United States entered World War II against Japan. Pei's father advised him to stay in the United States until the war ended.

So Pei stayed in the United States. He married Eileen Loo in 1942. And he took what he later called his most distasteful job. He worked for the National Defense Research Committee. His task was to find better ways to destroy enemy buildings.

After the war, Pei went back to school. He studied at Harvard University's Graduate School of Design. There, he studied with two famous German designers, Walter Gropius and Marcel Breuer. Breuer's ideas about "light, texture, sun, and shadow" were to become basic to all Pei's future work.

When Pei finished his master's degree, he hoped to return to China. Once again, his hopes were dashed. China had just been taken over by the Communists. Pei decided to stay in the United States.

In 1948, Pei was hired by a real estate developer in New York City. Pei designed and built many different kinds of projects for the developer. For each project, a slum area was cleared out. Then new buildings were built: private homes, office buildings, parks, shopping centers. Pei tried his hand at them all. What a wealth of experience for a young architect!

In 1954, Pei and his wife became U.S. citizens. By this time they had three sons. Later a daughter was born to them.

In 1955, Pei decided he was ready to start his own firm—I.M. Pei and Partners. He continued to work on city projects. His work was highly praised.

In the mid-1960's, Pei's work began to get more dramatic. One project gained him national attention: the National Center for Atmospheric Research in Boulder, Colorado, located in an isolated area. Pei chose to design the building as a group of reddish-brown towers that blended into the environment. They looked something like Indian pueblos framed by the Rocky Mountains.

In 1964, Jacqueline Kennedy chose Pei as the architect for the John F. Kennedy Library in Boston. Many better-known architects were considered before Pei was selected. The project turned out to be a hard one. Three times, the building site was changed. Each time Pei had to start over with the plans. Fifteen years later, the library opened. For his work, Pei received a gold medal from the American Institute of Architects.

Pei was gaining national fame. But not everything he touched did well. The John Hancock Building in Boston nearly cost Pei his business.

This building was designed by one of Pei's partners. The 60-story building was covered in blue-green glass. The glass looked like mirrors. There was only one problem. The huge windows began popping out and crashing to the ground far below. Over and over, the windows were replaced. And over and over, they fell back out.

Pei was in the headlines. But it was not good publicity. It took a long time before the trouble was discovered. The problem had to do with how the glass was made. All the windows had to be removed and replaced. In the meantime, Pei's business dropped off sharply.

Pei's image soon recovered. His East Building annex to the National Gallery of Art in Washington, D.C., was opened to huge acclaim. This striking building was made up of two triangles of pink marble and large glass skylights. Critics hailed the building as a triumph.

In the late 1970's, the United States and China resumed political relations. This led to two jobs that pleased Pei greatly. He was asked to design a hotel in Beijing, China. For this, he made his first trip back to China since leaving at the age of 17. Later, he designed an office building for the Bank of China.

In 1983, French President Mitterrand chose Pei for a big job in Paris, France. An addition was needed for the famous art museum, the Louvre. Offices, shops, parking space, and storage areas were needed at the museum.

The Louvre had been built in the 1200's. It was first a castle. In the 1700's, it was used as a palace by French kings. After the French Revolution, it became an art museum.

Pei studied the Louvre for a long time. He did not want his addition to interfere with the history of the original building. So, he decided to build a huge space, all underground, beneath the Louvre's huge courtyard. The addition was capped by a large glass pyramid and three smaller ones.

Many Parisians were astonished. But many more were outraged! How could Pei even think of putting such a modern structure in the middle of a classical building? The debate was loud and furious.

"Paris is made fun of," art critics roared. Pei's reply was simple. "On this pyramid, people will see the moving reflex of the clouds and the stars." Today, Parisians have accepted the pyramid. One official called it "an admirable jewel, turning the Louvre into the most beautiful museum in the world."

Many artists and architects develop a special style. Their work can be easily identified because their style remains the same from one project to another.

Pei is different because he has never developed a single style. He studies each project carefully. Then he designs an inventive structure to meet the needs of the project. He is truly a giant among architects.

Remembering the Facts

1. How did I.M. Pei develop his love of architecture as a child?

2. Why did Pei go to America?

3. Why couldn't Pei return to China after he finished his studies, as he had first planned to do?

4. What distasteful job did Pei have with the National Defense Research Committee?

5. What event in China prevented Pei from returning after World War II ended?

6. What work did Pei do for a real estate developer in New York City?

7. Which project nearly cost Pei his business?

8.   Name three major projects for which Pei is famous.

Understanding the Story

9.   Pei's work is creative and original. Why do you think an inventive artist would be likely to cause debate with his or her work?

10.   Why do you think most architects and artists develop a recognizable style?

Getting the Main Idea

Why do you think I.M. Pei is a giant among architects?

Applying What You've Learned

When I.M. Pei takes a job, he studies the site carefully. Then he designs a structure that fits the site and the needs of the job. Design a home you would like to live in. First choose a site you like. Think about how the home would fit on the site. Then make a sketch of your dream home. Make the most of the site you have chosen.

Maya Lin

Sculptor

When she was still a student, Maya Lin became one of the most controversial artists in the world. At first, many people did not like her design for the Vietnam Veterans Memorial in Washington, D.C. Now, it has become a beloved national shrine. More people visit this monument each year than any other in the entire country.

Lin was born in 1959 in Athens, Ohio. Her parents had come to America in the 1940's from China. Both taught at Ohio University. Her father was a ceramist and dean of the art school. Her mother was a poet and literature professor.

As a child, Maya enjoyed hiking, bird-watching, and reading. She also worked in her father's pottery studio. In high school, she worked at a McDonald's restaurant after school.

Maya Lin

She was a gifted student. She especially loved math and art. After high school, she went to Yale University.

At Yale, Maya Lin wanted to major in both sculpture and architecture. The school would not allow her to do this. So she enrolled in the architecture program. But she kept on taking sculpture classes.

In 1980, a nationwide contest was held to design the Vietnam Veterans Memorial. One of Lin's professors asked the students in his class to enter designs.

The memorial was to be built in Washington, D.C. The site was between the Lincoln Memorial and the Capitol.

Lin went to Washington to study the building site. The beautiful, grassy area gave her a peaceful, calm feeling. She knew she wanted to keep that feeling in her work.

Her final design was two long, black granite walls. The walls came together to form a giant V. On the wall were the names of the 58,000 men and women who were killed or missing in action in the war. The names were written in the order in which they died or were reported missing.

Over 1400 artists entered the competition. The names of the artists were not revealed to the judges.

On May 6, 1981, the winning entry was announced. It was Lin. At the time, she was a senior at Yale. And she was totally unknown in the art world.

Some Vietnam veterans were unhappy with the choice. They wanted a more traditional statue—perhaps something with soldiers on it. Her design was called a "wall of shame."

But it got worse. When the protesters found out that Lin was a Chinese-American woman, they were outraged. Many sexist and racist slurs were directed at her.

Lin was shocked and hurt. She had always thought of herself as just another American college student. She had never felt the sting of racial prejudice before.

In her own words:

"The competition was anonymous. No names were allowed on any of the boards. It has always been a question in my mind as to what would've happened if names had been allowed. I hope sometime that people's names can be left on and it won't make a difference . . ." (as quoted in *The Chinese Americans*).

The debate went on for nearly a year. Finally, a compromise was reached. The wall would be built as Lin had designed it. But a more traditional monument would be added near the entrance to the memorial site.

The Vietnam Veterans Memorial was dedicated on November 13, 1982. Lin's name was not even mentioned during the ceremony.

But all that changed as people began visiting the memorial. Thousands came to find the names of their loved ones killed in the war. Many made rubbings of the engraved names. The memorial became a place of healing.

In 1987, Lin was asked to design a memorial in Montgomery, Alabama, for those who had died in the civil rights struggle. She began studying the civil rights movement. She read the works of Dr. Martin Luther King, Jr.

In 1963, Dr. King had given his famous "I have a dream" speech. In that speech, King said, "We will not be satisfied . . . until justice rolls down like waters and righteousness like a mighty stream." Lin was inspired by the image of rolling water.

She designed the monument in two parts. First there was a black granite disk about 12 feet across. On it were written 21 important events in the civil rights movement. Forty people who died in the struggle were listed.

Behind the disk was the second part of the monument. It was a nine-foot wall with King's quotation engraved on it. Both pieces were covered with a thin sheet of very slowly moving water.

The Civil Rights Memorial was dedicated in 1989. Lin was surprised and moved when people began to cry during the ceremony. Again she had created a place where healing could take place.

Her fame was spreading. During the 1990's Lin completed a number of different projects.

Yale University asked her to design a sculpture to honor women at the school. Lin's design was a three-foot-high table of green granite. Water seeped through a hole in the center of the table.

On top of the table was a spiral of numbers. The numbers showed how many women were enrolled at Yale for each year since the college was founded in 1701.

But no women were allowed into Yale for almost 200 years after it was founded. So the center of the spiral was filled with zeros. Thus, *The Women's Table* commented on the many years of discrimination against women at Yale.

In 1993, Lin completed remodeling a building to house the Museum of African Art in New York City. She also did a sculpture called *Groundswell* for Ohio State University.

In 1994, Lin designed a 14-foot-long clock for Pennsylvania Station in New York City. It is made of clear glass. It is lit by hundreds of fiber-optic points of light.

Lin has become an important American artist. Perhaps her greatest works are her monuments. They have helped heal the wounds of the Vietnam War and the civil rights struggle. Lin is still a young woman. She will no doubt have many more contributions to make to American art.

Remembering the Facts

1.   What two subjects did Maya Lin like best at Yale?

2.   Why did Lin enter the Vietnam Veterans Memorial design competition?

3.   What did her winning entry look like?

4.   Name two reasons some people did not like her design.

5.   What compromise was reached before the memorial could be built?

6.   Why did people's ideas about the memorial change after they saw it?

7.   What was the purpose of the memorial Lin designed for Montgomery, Alabama?

8.   Where did Lin find her inspiration for that memorial?

9.   What comment does *The Women's Table* make about the role of women at Yale University?

Understanding the Story

10.   The Vietnam Veterans Memorial has been said to look like a row of black headstones. In what ways do you think the memorial could be compared to a cemetery?

11.   Do you think Lin would have won the competition if the judges had known she was Chinese American? Why or why not?

Getting the Main Idea

How do you think Maya Lin's work has helped heal wounds from two difficult times in our country's history: the Vietnam War and the civil rights struggle?

Applying What You've Learned

Design your own sculpture (on paper) using the words "I have a dream . . . " from Dr. Martin Luther King, Jr.'s famous speech. Your work should show a dream you have for our country.

An Wang

Inventor

An Wang was an inventor and the founder of Wang Laboratories. Wang started his company with just $600. It grew to become one of the largest companies in the United States.

An Wang

Wang was the second of five children. He was born in Shanghai, China, in 1920. He grew up in the 1920's and 1930's during a time in China's history called the Age of Confusion. Warlords fought each other for power. Later, Japan invaded the country. Finally, the Communists fought the Nationalists. All this fighting caused hunger and bloodshed all over the country. It was not an easy time to grow up.

Wang's father was an English teacher. When Wang was six, his family moved to Kun San. The school where Wang's father was teaching had no kindergarten, first, or second grade. So, Wang began school as a third-grader at age six.

For the rest of his years of school, Wang was two years younger than his schoolmates. He later said it was a little bit like being thrown in the water when you don't know how to swim. You either learn how to swim—and fast—or you sink.

After school, Wang's grandmother taught him about Chinese literature and thought. She taught him the ideas of Confucius, a famous Chinese philosopher. From his grandmother, Wang learned ways he kept all his life: moderation, patience, balance, and simplicity.

In school, Wang found math easy. But he had trouble in classes that did not interest him. His grades in some classes were so poor, he barely graduated from sixth grade.

It was not easy for students to go to junior high school in China. Only 50 to 100 students were chosen each year from a city of 100,000 people. Students had to take an exam to get in. Wang's parents did not think he should take the exam because his grades were so poor. But he did. And he got the highest score of any student that year.

At 13, Wang went to high school. It was a boarding school 10 miles out of Shanghai. The textbooks were in English. This made things very hard. But later, when he came to the United States, he found he was well prepared.

One problem with being younger than everyone else was being too small to do well in sports. Wang tried being a goalie in soccer. He once said he felt more like a target than a goalie. Then he discovered table tennis. In this sport, size was not so important. He later became good enough to play on his university team.

At 16, Wang went to Chiao Tung University in Shanghai. This school was known as the MIT of China. Since Wang had the highest college entrance exam scores of his class, he was named class president. He kept that job for four years. His major in college was electrical engineering.

During his first year of college, his mother died. She had not been directly killed by the ongoing wars. But Wang felt that her health had been broken by the years of fear and conflict.

In 1937, the Japanese invaded China and seized Peking (Beijing). War was everywhere. But the university had moved to a zone under French control. Neither army was allowed to enter the

French zone. Wang graduated from college in 1940 to the sound of Japanese shells whistling overhead.

In 1941, Wang and eight classmates signed up for a Chinese government project. They would design and build transmitters and radios for government troops.

Wang called this project a "seat-of-the-pants" operation. The group never knew what parts they might be able to get. They learned to make do and use what they could scrounge up. Several times a week, they were interrupted by Japanese bombing raids. The team waited out these raids in nearby caves. There they passed the time playing cards. During this time, Wang's father and older sister were killed in the fighting.

Finally, in 1945, the war ended. The Chinese government decided to send a group of Chinese engineers to the United States. The idea was to train them to help rebuild China. They would go to American companies and watch and learn from them. Then they would bring their knowledge back to China.

Wang entered this program. He arrived in the United States in 1945. He decided that going to school could teach him more than observing in an American company. So, he enrolled at Harvard. In 1948, he completed his Ph.D. in applied physics.

By this time, the Communists had taken over in China. Wang decided he could not return to his homeland.

He took a position with Howard Aiken in the Harvard Computation Laboratory. Aiken had designed the first binary computer in the United States to be operated by electricity. It was called the Mark I. This huge computer was 51 feet long and 8 feet high.

Wang was asked to figure out a way to increase the speed at which the computer could access memory. Dr. Wang invented "memory cores" to do this. These memory cores were to become a staple for computer memory for the next 20 years.

While working at Harvard, Wang met his future wife, Lorraine Chu. They were married and later had three children.

Wang decided to start his own business. He would make and sell memory cores as well as work on other projects in his field. He began with $600 in savings and one loyal employee—himself. He worked on a number of small projects. Then in 1956, he sold his memory core invention to IBM for $400,000.

Wang invented a number of different electronic products. But it was the desktop calculator that made Wang Labs a giant. The company's first calculator was called the LOCI. It could add, subtract, multiply, divide, do square roots, and figure exponential values—all at a cost of $6500

A year later, a second desktop calculator was introduced. It cost only $1695. Sales were booming. Wang Labs was a million-dollar business employing over 400 people by 1967.

Wang continued to invent new products. In 1971, he invented the first word-processing typewriter. In 1976, he brought out a word-processing system using computer screens and menus to guide the user.

Today, Wang Laboratories is a Fortune 500 company with 30,000 employees. Sales top $5 billion a year. Wang himself led the company until his death in 1990.

Wang became the fifth richest man in the United States. Yet he never lost his basic values. He lived a quiet, family-oriented life-style. In fact, he never owned more than two suits at a time.

In his autobiography, Wang said that "all of us owe the world more than we received when we were born." So, he gave money to worthy causes in health care, education, and the arts. He chose projects in the same way he ran his business "to find a need and fill it."

At MIT, Wang funded a program that helped engineers from China come to the United States to study. He endowed the Wang Center in Boston, a performing arts center. He built an outpatient clinic at Massachusetts General Hospital. He began the Wang Insti tute to provide training in computer science and business. He also built a $15 million computer plant to provide jobs in Boston's Chinatown.

In 1986, Wang received one of the greatest honors of his life. He was awarded the Medal of Liberty. This award was given during a ceremony for the relighting of the Statue of Liberty torch. It was given to 12 Americans born abroad who had made their mark in America.

Wang said in his autobiography: "It is a mark of the generosity of the American spirit that the nation would choose to honor the contributions of its newest rather than its oldest citizens." Wang's contributions to American life were great.

Remembering the Facts

1. What was the Age of Confusion?

2. Why was An Wang younger than his classmates?

3. Name two values Wang's grandmother taught him.

4. What did Wang study in college?

5. What project did Wang work on in 1941?

6. How did Wang end up going to the United States?

7. Why did Wang decide he couldn't return to China?

8. What invention did Wang sell to IBM for $400,000?

9. What invention made Wang Labs a giant company?

10. Name two ways Wang "gave back" to his community.

Understanding the Story

11. As a child, Wang lived through war and the loss of both parents and one sister. He said in his autobiography, *Lessons*, that "confidence is sometimes rooted in the unpleasant aspects of life. The longer you are able to survive and succeed, the better you are able to further survive and succeed." What do you think he meant by this? Do you agree or disagree?

12. An Wang's name means "peaceful king." In what ways do you think his name fit him?

Getting the Main Idea

On July 3, 1986, Wang was awarded the Medal of Liberty as one of 12 outstanding citizens who had been born in another country. Why do you think Wang was chosen for this award?

Applying What You've Learned

Wang's philosophy was "to find a need and fill it." Think of a need in your school, home, or community. What would be a good way to fill that need? Write a paragraph describing your project.

Haing Ngor

Physician and Actor

Beautiful movie actresses. Handsome actors. Gold, glitter, wealth. All of Hollywood's "beautiful people" had gathered in one spot. It was Academy Awards night, 1985.

Dressed in a tux and shiny patent leather shoes, Haing Ngor waited. Then he heard his name called. Haing Ngor had won an Oscar for Best Supporting Actor for his role as Dith Pran in *The Killing Fields.*

Haing Ngor

As he stepped to the stage to receive his Oscar, his mind went back six years—to a different life halfway around the globe in Cambodia.

Ngor was proud to win an Academy Award. But he knew that "his best performances were over before he left Cambodia. And the prize there was much greater."

Ngor was born sometime around 1950 in Cambodia. His earliest memory as a child was standing in the doorway of his parents' home in the small village of Samrong Yong. There he could see out over the rice fields. It was peaceful and beautiful.

31

Yet even then, there was trouble in the land. One day when Ngor was three, his mother sent him and his brother to get water from a pond. On the way back, shooting broke out behind them. He and his family hid in a hole lined with sandbags in the floor of their home. When the shooting stopped, one guerrilla soldier lay dead in the family's front yard. It was a sign of much worse things yet to come.

Cambodia had been ruled by the French for nearly 100 years. But now, guerrillas were rebelling against French rule. The people of Cambodia were caught in the middle of the struggle for power. Ngor's parents were kidnapped by one side, then the other. Each time, they were released when a ransom was paid.

The Ngor family had eight children, five boys and three girls. The father owned a store in the village of Samrong Yong. Later, he owned a trucking business and a lumber mill.

Ngor's father wanted him to work in the family business. But Ngor wanted to go to medical school. Finally, his father gave him permission.

Ngor began his training in the capital city of Phnom Penh. It would take seven years in all. To support himself, Ngor began tutoring high school students. One of his students was Chang My Huoy, who later became his wife.

There were not enough doctors in Cambodia. So students were allowed to practice medicine before they got their degree. Ngor worked long hours in clinics and hospitals, in addition to going to school. In February 1975, he got his degree. His specialty was obstetrics and gynecology (delivering babies and treating women).

Ngor was living well. He bought a Mercedes for himself and another one for Huoy. They ate in luxury restaurants every night.

But all around them, war was raging. To the east, in Vietnam, the United States and the Vietcong fought a war neither side could win. To the west, in Thailand, the United States based its warplanes. To the north, in Laos, the Communists and royalists battled. In the middle of all this was Cambodia, a small country about the size of Washington state.

Cambodia had been at peace because of its popular leader, Prince Norodom Sihanouk. But in 1970, Sihanouk's government was overthrown. General Lon Nol led the coup.

Then, in the early 1970's, a Communist group called the Khmer Rouge began fighting Lon Nol's government. The group gained strength and began to overrun the country. By 1975, they were approaching Phnom Penh.

Most of the people living in Phnom Penh were not worried about the Khmer Rouge. As Ngor said, "The Khmer Rouge were Communists, but they were also Cambodians. Cambodians wouldn't hurt each other without a reason. That's what I believed, and that's what my friends were saying, too."

On April 17, 1975, the city fell to the Khmer Rouge. Ngor was at his clinic. He was operating on a man who had been hit by a grenade. Suddenly, the door to the operating room burst open. A Khmer Rouge guerrilla ran in and put a gun to Ngor's head. He demanded to know if Ngor was a doctor. Sensing danger, Ngor said that the doctor had left by the back door minutes ago. The guerrilla, who was about 12 years old, ran out. Ngor and his staff fled. The patient was left on the table to die.

The Khmer Rouge made everyone leave the city. Tens of thousands of people filled the streets, trudging out of the city. They all carried what they could. The rich pushed handcarts. The poor carried nothing but their rice pots. The Cambodian revolution had begun.

For the next four years, Ngor lived through unbelievable conditions. Everyone was forced to work in labor camps under primitive conditions. There was very little food. People were killed at the whim of the Khmer Rouge. Doctors and teachers were prime targets. So, Ngor hid his true identity, claiming to be a taxi driver.

The harsh conditions in the labor camps began to take their toll. Food was scarce. The people were not allowed to search for wild food (although they tried to secretly). There were no latrines. Drinking water was unclean. There was no medicine. And the people had to labor long hours in the fields.

It wasn't long before people began dying in huge numbers. More than one million people died during the four-year period. Both Ngor's parents and most of his brothers and sisters died. Ngor himself nearly died when his weight dropped to 70 pounds. He was saved from death when his wife found a yam to feed him.

The Khmer Rouge also began a campaign of torture. Once Ngor was accused of hiding food. Half of his little finger was cut off as punishment. Another time he was accused of being a doctor. The Khmer Rouge hung him over a slow fire for four days.

In 1978, Ngor's wife was pregnant. She went into labor early. Weak from near starvation, she did not have the strength to recover. Ngor had no medicine and no medical equipment. So, he was unable to save her, even with his medical training. Both she and the child died.

In 1979, Ngor was able to escape to Thailand. There, he worked for a year, treating other Cambodian refugees. Then in 1980, he was allowed to leave for the United States, along with other refugees. He ended up in Los Angeles.

Ngor could not practice medicine in the United States. So he took a job helping other refugees find work. One day, a person casting a movie about Cambodia spotted Ngor. He was hired to act in *The Killing Fields.*

The movie was about a *New York Times* correspondent and his Cambodian assistant, Dith Pran. It would show the horrors Dith Pran lived through under the Khmer Rouge. When Ngor was hired, no one had any idea how much his own life was like the story of Dith Pran.

The Killing Fields was released in 1984 to rave reviews. Ngor became rich and famous. He used his new position in the spotlight to tell the world about Cambodia. In 1987, he wrote his autobiography, called *A Cambodian Odyssey.*

Ngor traveled the country, giving lectures and promoting his book. Nearly all the money he made was given to help refugee children around the world.

Ngor survived the killing fields of Cambodia only to die on the streets of Los Angeles. On February 25, 1996, he was shot to death in front of his Chinatown home. The reason for his senseless death was unknown.

Remembering the Facts

1. For what movie did Haing Ngor win an Oscar in 1985 (for his role as Dith Pran)?

2. How did Ngor meet his future wife?

3. Where did Ngor go to medical school?

4. Why were medical students allowed to practice medicine while they were still in school?

5. Who led the coup that overthrew the Sihanouk government in 1970?

6. What happened on April 17, 1975, that changed Ngor's life?

7. Give three reasons why so many people died under the Khmer Rouge.

8. Where did Ngor go to escape the Khmer Rouge?

9. How did Ngor use the fame he gained from winning the Academy Award?

10. What did Ngor do with most of the money he earned?

Understanding the Story

11. When Ngor won the Academy Award, he said that his "best performances were over before he left Cambodia. And the prize there was much greater." What do you think he meant?

12. Before the fall of Phnom Penh, Ngor had an opportunity to leave the country and continue his medical studies in France. He chose not to do this. Why do you think he stayed in Cambodia?

Getting the Main Idea

What important lessons do you think can be learned from the story of Haing Ngor?

Applying What You've Learned

People may become refugees because of war or natural disasters in their country. How do you think individuals can help these refugees?

Seiji Ozawa

Symphony Conductor

Seiji Ozawa

Seiji Ozawa has been the much-admired conductor of the Boston Symphony Orchestra for over 20 years. His music has brought pleasure to millions around the world.

Ozawa was born in 1935 to Japanese parents. The family lived in Manchuria, China, an area that was occupied by Japanese troops at that time.

Ozawa's father, Kaisaku Ozawa, was a dentist. He believed that all Asians should live as brothers. Kaisaku joined a pacifist group. He helped publish an antiwar newsletter.

Kaisaku's views were not popular with the Japanese government. So, in 1941, the family was deported to Japan. They moved to a military air base near Tokyo called Tachikawa.

Kaisaku was not allowed to practice dentistry in Japan. So the family lived in poverty.

On December 7, 1941, the Japanese bombed Pearl Harbor in Hawaii. The United States entered World War II. At this time, Ozawa was six years old.

Thus, Ozawa's childhood was shaped by war. In some ways, his life was like that of any other six-year-old's. He went to school every day, and he played with his friends.

But the war put a shadow over his childhood. The nearby air base was often attacked by bombers. When the air-raid signal sounded, all the children had to go home from school and hide in underground shelters. The school had no bomb shelters.

The war went on and on. There was little food. Ozawa's mother mixed grass into the family's rice to make it go further. Ozawa's best friend was killed when his house was destroyed by a bomb.

Ozawa saw his first American when he was 10 years old. He was swimming with friends in the river. A low-flying bomber flew by on its way to bomb a nearby factory. The plane came so close, Ozawa could see right into the cockpit.

On August 7, 1945, an atomic bomb was dropped on the Japanese city of Hiroshima. In a flash, 180,000 Japanese were killed or wounded. The destruction was terrifying. Two days later, a second bomb was dropped on Nagasaki.

Then announcements came over the radio. American soldiers were coming! The soldiers were described as terrible beasts. Children were urged to make spears from bamboo to get ready to defend themselves.

Japan could endure no more. They were forced to surrender. V-J Day (Victory in Japan Day) was celebrated in America. But in Japan, the people readied themselves for an American takeover.

Ozawa described his feelings as General MacArthur and his troops entered the country. "When the Americans came in, it was a very emotional time for us and a big surprise for the children. Instead of the monsters we had been taught about, there were all these happy young people with chewing gum. . . . I never go past the chewing gum displays in the supermarket and smell it without thinking about that day." (from the *Boston Globe*)

After the war ended, life became more normal for the Ozawa family. Kaisaku Ozawa, still a pacifist, was thrilled. Now the family could pursue more interests. The Ozawas became rice farmers.

Seiji Ozawa became interested in music. But everyone was surprised when he said he wanted to learn to play the piano. All the other children were learning to play traditional Japanese instruments.

Ozawa's parents found a piano teacher for him in Tokyo, where the family had moved in 1944. Ozawa showed talent for the instrument. In 1953, he was accepted at the Toho School of Music in Tokyo.

Another of Ozawa's interests was soccer. When he was 19 years old, he broke both of his index fingers during a soccer game. For eight months, he was unable to play the piano. So, in the meantime, he took up the study of conducting.

Ozawa graduated from the Toho School of Music in 1959. He conducted the Japan Philharmonic Orchestra that year. He did so well, he was named the outstanding talent of the year.

After graduation, Ozawa decided he wanted to go to Europe to study further. He had no money. But that did not slow him down for long.

First, he talked a Japanese motor-scooter company into giving him one of their scooters. He would ride it around Europe as an advertising scheme. He earned his fare to Europe by working on a freighter. He arrived in Italy and rode the scooter to Paris. By this time, he had less than $100 to his name.

Ozawa earned some money by winning contests for young conductors. For the next two years, he studied in Paris and Berlin with famous conductors.

While he was studying in Berlin, Leonard Bernstein came to the city. He was the conductor of the famous New York Philharmonic Orchestra.

Bernstein had heard of the promising young Seiji Ozawa. After listening to him conduct, he offered Ozawa a job. He would be assistant conductor with the New York Philharmonic. Ozawa made his debut with the orchestra in 1961 at Carnegie Hall.

Ozawa returned to Japan in 1963. There he worked as musical director of Tokyo's Nisei Theater. He also worked with an opera company.

In 1965, Ozawa began a three-year job as conductor of the Toronto Symphony Orchestra. This was followed by five years with the San Francisco Symphony.

In 1973, Ozawa became conductor of the Boston Symphony Orchestra. He continues to hold this position today.

In the more than 20 years Ozawa has led the orchestra, he has gained worldwide attention. He has gained the love and admiration of the Boston public as well.

On July 7, 1994, there was a gala opening concert at a new concert hall at Tanglewood. The name of the hall was the Seiji Ozawa Concert Hall. This beautiful brick and timber building was a fitting tribute to Ozawa and his work.

For the 1994–1995 symphony season, Ozawa undertook a year-long series of concerts commemorating the fiftieth anniversary of the end of World War II. The special concerts contained music either written during the war or about the war. As a Japanese

American, Ozawa played a symbolic role in these programs. He led concerts in Berlin, Vienna, Nagasaki, and Tokyo.

Ozawa hoped that these programs would show how music is the universal language. He offered them as a memorial to all victims of the war, no matter what their nationality. Like his father before him, Ozawa is a man of peace.

Remembering the Facts

1. Why was the Ozawa family deported from China?

2. Why was the Ozawa family poor?

3. What event in 1945 brought World War II to a rapid end?

4. Why was Ozawa so surprised when the Americans arrived in his town?

5. How did Ozawa's love of soccer end his piano-playing career?

6. How did Ozawa earn enough money for his first trip to Europe?

7. What famous conductor gave Ozawa his big break?

8. What position has Ozawa held for over 20 years?

9. What is the name of the Tanglewood concert hall that opened in 1994?

10. What event did Ozawa commemorate in the 1994–1995 symphony season?

Understanding the Story

11. Why do you think Kaisaku Ozawa's pacifist activities were so unpopular with the Japanese government in 1941?

12. What events from Ozawa's childhood do you think shaped him into a pacifist?

Getting the Main Idea

What is the importance of Seiji Ozawa's contribution to American life?

Applying What You've Learned

Music has been called the universal language. Make a list of some music that makes you feel peaceful.

Kristi Yamaguchi

Figure Skater

Kristi Yamaguchi's childhood dream came true. In 1992, she won an Olympic gold medal in women's figure skating.

Yamaguchi was born in 1971 in Hayward, California. She grew up mainly in nearby Fremont. She was one of three children. Her father was a dentist. Her mother worked as a medical technician.

During World War II, Yamaguchi's parents and grandparents were held in internment camps, along with thousands of other Japanese Americans. But they were not bitter about the experience. They taught their children to be proud to be Americans. Yamaguchi's grandfather was proud to see her competing as an Asian American.

Kristi Yamaguchi

Yamaguchi was born with clubfeet. To take care of the problem, she had to wear corrective shoes. The shoes did the trick. Her feet were straightened. She had no further problems.

In 1976, five-year-old Yamaguchi sat glued to her television screen. She was watching Dorothy Hamill as she skated her way to an Olympic gold medal.

Hamill was very popular with the American public. She was seen in newspaper and television ads. Her bobbed haircut became the rage.

Hamill's skating set something ablaze in Yamaguchi. She decided that very day that she would win an Olympic gold medal, just as her heroine had.

There was only one problem. Yamaguchi didn't know how to skate. But it didn't take her long to talk her parents into letting her take lessons. And it didn't take long for her coach to discover that she had a natural talent.

When she was eight, she entered her first competition. By the time she was nine, she was getting up at 4:00 A.M. every day. She practiced for hours before going to school.

At this point, Yamaguchi began training with singles coach Christy Kjarsgaard-Ness. The two began a close working relationship that would last for many years.

When she was 12, Yamaguchi began working on pairs skating. In pairs skating, a man and woman skate together in a dancelike routine.

Yamaguchi's partner was Rudi Galindo. The two skaters worked with coach Jim Hulick. It was not long before they began winning fame. In 1985, they finished fifth in the National Junior Championships. By the next year, they had improved a lot. They finished in first place.

Yamaguchi was also improving as a singles skater. In 1988, she won gold medals in both the singles and pairs categories at the

World Junior Championships. She was named the Up and Coming Artistic Athlete of the Year by the Women's Sports Foundation.

In 1989, Yamaguchi won her first senior title. She and Galindo won the gold medal in the pairs competition at the National Championships. Yamaguchi also placed second in the singles division. She became the first woman in 35 years to win two medals at the nationals.

At that time, singles-skating competitions had two parts. First were the compulsory figures. In this event, the skater had to trace patterns on the ice, first with one foot and then the other. The skaters were judged by how well their skate marks matched the etched patterns. This was Yamaguchi's weakest event and the reason she came in second in singles.

The second part of singles competition was the free-skating section. Yamaguchi's free-skating performance dazzled the audience. She performed one of the most technically difficult routines in the world. And her technical expertise was matched by her artistry. Experts agreed that she was one of the most exciting figure skaters in years.

Because she performed so well at the nationals, Yamaguchi went on to her first World Championship Competition in 1989. At this meet, she finished in sixth place in singles. She and Rudi Galindo placed fifth in the pairs event.

It was clear that Yamaguchi was well on her way to a spot on the 1992 Olympic Figure Skating Team. The Olympics were just three years away. Those three years turned out to be a very difficult time in Yamaguchi's life.

Kjarsgaard-Ness, Yamaguchi's longtime coach, moved to Edmonton, Alberta. So, the day after her high-school graduation, Yamaguchi followed her coach to Canada. Galindo also moved to Edmonton. But their pairs coach, Hulick, was still in California. The two skaters were forced to commute between California and Canada. This soon became exhausting.

Then at the end of 1989, Hulick died of cancer. Yamaguchi and Galindo could not find another coach they liked. Finally, Yamaguchi decided to quit pairs skating and give singles her all.

Yamaguchi had some good luck, too. In July of 1990, the compulsory figures were taken out of all major competitions. Now Yamaguchi could work just on her free-skating program.

In the 1991 National Championships, Yamaguchi came in second. She was disappointed, but focused on winning at the World Competition that was coming up. It worked. Yamaguchi came in first.

At last, it was time for the Olympics. The 1992 Winter Games were to be held in Albertville, France. The press picked Yamaguchi to take second place. They thought Midori Ito of Japan would win first place. Ito was the only woman in the world to have landed the difficult triple axel.

As it turned out, Yamaguchi was lucky to be entering the games as the underdog. This took a lot of the pressure to win off her. Yamaguchi marched in the opening ceremonies. She stayed in the Olympic Village and went dancing with the other athletes. Meanwhile, her rival Midori Ito was practicing hard on her routines.

Yamaguchi's relaxed attitude came through on the ice, too. Her rivals made mistake after mistake. Yamaguchi glided through her short program as though all she wanted to do was to please her audience. Two days later, she presented an almost flawless long program.

Kristi Yamaguchi realized a dream she had worked for since childhood: She won an Olympic gold medal.

In September 1992, Yamaguchi decided to turn professional. That meant she could no longer compete in the World Championships or the Olympic Games. But she would be free to earn money from her skating.

Many business experts thought that Yamaguchi would not be offered the chance to endorse products as other superstars do.

They thought that she would not appeal to people because she is a Japanese American. Happily, they were proved wrong.

Yamaguchi signed contracts with the Kellogg Company and a number of other companies. She appeared in television ads and in magazines. She even appeared in a movie, *D2: The Mighty Ducks.* Yamaguchi is now skating as part of the Discover Card "Stars on Ice" tour.

Yamaguchi hasn't let fame go to her head. She told *Sports Illustrated*, "It's still funny to have other people fussing over your hair, pretending you're a model for a day. I still feel I'm the same old kid, and someone who still wants to be one."

Remembering the Facts

1. What gold medal winner inspired Kristi Yamaguchi to become a figure skater?

2. How did Yamaguchi find time to practice skating during the school year?

3. Why was Christy Kjarsgaard-Ness important in Yamaguchi's career?

4. Who was Yamaguchi's pairs partner?

5. What are compulsory figures?

6. Why was entering the Olympics as an underdog good for Yamaguchi?

7. What does it mean when skaters turn professional?

8. Why did many business experts think Yamaguchi would not be offered endorsement contracts?

9. What work is Yamaguchi doing now?

Understanding the Story

10. What do you think are some of the sacrifices skaters might have to make to succeed in winning a gold medal?

11. Which do you think is more important in the making of a world-class athlete: natural talent or hard work? Why?

Getting the Main Idea

Why do you think Kristi Yamaguchi is a good role model for young people of today?

Applying What You've Learned

Create a drawing to advertise a product used by teenagers. Choose a famous person to endorse the product.

Noriyuki "Pat" Morita

Actor

Noriyuki "Pat" Morita is a movie star. He is best known as the karate master in *The Karate Kid* series. But Morita's own life would make an exciting movie. He calls his life a series of Cinderella stories.

Noriyuki "Pat" Morita

Morita was born in 1933 in Isleton, California. His parents came to California from Japan in the early part of the century. His father was a migrant farmworker.

When Morita was two years old, he became ill with spinal tuberculosis. He was not expected to live to see his third birthday. Morita was taken from his family and sent to a hospital for patients with tuberculosis. There, he spent the next nine years in a body cast from his shoulders to his knees. He stayed in bed, unable to walk.

While he was in the hospital, Morita was often visited by a priest. The two became friends. The priest gave Morita the nickname Pat. The name stuck.

Finally, an operation brought a cure. At age 11, Morita learned to walk. He was released from the hospital.

But he did not get to go home. It was 1943, the middle of the World War II years. Japanese Americans had been relocated away from the West Coast. The Morita family had been sent to Tulelake Internment Center in the Arizona desert.

Morita told *People* magazine, "One day, I was an invalid. The next day, I was an 11-year-old Public Enemy No. 1, escorted to an internment camp by the FBI." Now, Morita was getting a taste of racial discrimination.

The United States military feared that some Japanese Americans might secretly be loyal to Japan. They worried that if there were a Japanese invasion of the West Coast, these people might sabotage our country. The military decided all Japanese Americans should be put where they could be watched. This was done, even though two thirds of these people were American citizens.

This precaution turned out to be unnecessary. Japanese Americans proved their loyalty over and over. The combat record of Japanese Americans in the United States forces was outstanding, especially in the 442nd Infantry Regimental Combat Team. (See the story on Senator Daniel Inouye, pages 1–5.)

It was a very hard time for Japanese Americans. First, they were forced to leave their homes and businesses. Then, they were shut up behind barbed wire. There was also the hurt of being locked up just because of one's race.

It was harder on the older people than on the young. Although they were American citizens, they had been stripped of their civil rights. At the same time they were locked up, many of their sons were fighting in the United States armed forces.

Some of those interned committed suicide. Others became mentally ill. But most kept their sanity by gardening and by telling jokes and stories.

When the war ended in 1945, the Moritas were released. They settled in Fairfield, near Sacramento. Morita finished high school. He married and had a daughter. And he went to work in his father's Chinese restaurant. Morita told *The Daily Oklahoman*, "It was a

Japanese family running a Chinese restaurant in a black and Filipino neighborhood."

Morita's father was killed in a hit-and-run accident. The family could not hold on to the restaurant. So Morita began working in the computer department at Aerojet-General Corporation. He began as a shift supervisor and rose to department head. It was a secure job. But Morita was restless.

At 30, Morita was trying to figure out what he really wanted to do with his life. He kept coming back to the idea of getting into show business.

Morita says he got into comedy by default. He wasn't handsome enough to be a leading man. He couldn't sing or dance. But he was good at telling stories and making up jokes. He had done plenty of both in his long years in the hospital and the internment camp.

Morita's marriage did not survive the career change. He remarried in 1970. He and his second wife have two daughters.

Morita spent his first decade in show business as a stand-up comic in nightclubs. Mostly, he came on as an opening act for big-name performers. He also did some television commercials and bit parts in movies.

In 1973, Morita landed the role of Arnold, a hamburger shop owner, in the hit television show *Happy Days*. As Arnold, Morita was playing another "funny Japanese American." But the role brought him national recognition.

Two years later, Morita was given a starring role in his own television series, *Mr. T. and Tina*. The show was not a success. It lasted less than one season. But Morita was the first Japanese American to star in his own television series.

The next few years were hard for Morita. A storm totally destroyed his uninsured home. His mother-in-law died of cancer. Then his daughter came down with a serious illness. He wasn't doing well in his career either. Jobs were few and far between. Morita thought about giving up show business.

Then, in 1984, Morita was hired for the part of Miyagi, the karate master in *The Karate Kid*. Miyagi was Morita's first dramatic role. It was also his first chance to play a real Japanese character instead of a comic role. In the movie credits, Morita used his real Japanese name: Noriyuki. He did this to honor his parents and his Japanese roots. For the role of Miyagi, Morita was nominated for an Oscar for best supporting actor.

The success of *The Karate Kid* surprised everyone, including Morita. He thought it would be a short-lived summer show. The movie ended up earning over $100 million. In 1986, *The Karate Kid, Part II* was released. Then, in 1989, there was *Karate Kid III*. The series continued with *The Next Karate Kid* in 1994. Are more *Karate Kids* in store for us? Only time will tell.

Morita thinks *The Karate Kid* was a success because it was "a welcome relief" to people. In so many movies, the heroes use guns to wipe out all the problems in their lives. "Then along comes Miyagi, who fights with compassion and understanding and knowledge. Those are the things that most people have to fight with." (from *People* magazine)

Morita thinks that Miyagi represents a father figure. Many youngsters grow up without a strong father figure in their lives. Miyagi is a strong character with rock-solid values. This type of person is not often seen in movies anymore.

There is a scene in *The Karate Kid* where Miyagi tries to catch flies with a pair of chopsticks. The effort takes both discipline and patience. These are qualities Morita has in abundance. He credits his parents with giving him a strong work ethic, a stubborn persistence, and a good sense of humor. Sometimes, that is just what you need to make it in life!

Remembering the Facts

1. What illness caused Morita to be in a hospital for nine years as a child?

2. Where did Morita go when he was released from the hospital at age 11?

3. Why did the United States military think it was necessary to set up internment camps?

4. Why did the Morita family lose their Chinese restaurant?

5. Why did Morita quit his job at Aerojet-General and change careers?

6. Why did Morita start doing comedy shows?

7. What role did Morita play in the television show *Happy Days*?

8. What television show made Morita the first Japanese American to star in his own program?

9. How was the role of Miyagi in *The Karate Kid* different from any role Morita had played before?

10. Why does Morita think *The Karate Kid* was such a success with both children and adults?

Understanding the Story

11. Why do you think the United States government felt justified in placing Japanese-American citizens in internment camps during World War II?

12. After World War II ended, the government paid Japanese Americans for some of their suffering and losses of property during

the relocation. Why do you think that money could never completely make up for their losses?

Getting the Main Idea

Pat Morita is not a bitter man. He says, "My life has been a series of Cinderella stories." What do you think he means by this?

Applying What You've Learned

Imagine that you are a Japanese-American teenager who has been relocated with your family to an internment camp in the Arizona desert. Write a paragraph describing your feelings at being taken from your home and confined to the camp.

Yo-Yo Ma

Cellist

Yo-Yo Ma

Yo-Yo Ma is known as the best cellist playing today. He has played the cello for 36 of his 40 years. Since his early childhood, Ma has amazed the musical world.

Ma was born in Paris, France, in 1955. His father was a violinist who came to Paris from mainland China in 1936 to study music. Ma's mother was a gifted singer. She moved to Paris in 1949. There the two met and were married. They had two children.

The Mas began teaching their children while they were very young. They had two ways of teaching. Ma's father taught the children to analyze and study each piece of music. His mother, on the other hand, showed them the beauty and emotional side of music. Ma's playing is a combination of these approaches.

Ma's first instrument was the violin. But his older sister was learning to play the violin, too. So he decided he wanted to do something else. He didn't really care what. But he wanted it to be "something bigger." So the four-year-old boy decided to play the cello.

But a cello was much bigger than young Ma. So his father made one for him. He put an end pin on a viola so it would stand up. The boy still could not reach. So five telephone books were stacked on a chair. Then the lessons began.

Ma's father was a good teacher. His method was simple. He broke down musical works into small, easy-to-learn pieces. Each day, the child would learn two measures of music. Then those two measures were added to what he had already learned. Ma later said that it was no strain at all.

Ma's father did not believe in long hours of practicing either. He made young Ma practice only five to ten minutes a day. But when he did practice, he had to do it with great concentration.

By the time he was five years old, Ma could play three Bach cello suites by heart. That same year, he gave his first public recital at the University of Paris. A star was born!

When Ma was six, the family moved to New York. His father had been hired to teach at a school for musically gifted children. A number of famous musicians had children attending the school. Young Ma was soon noticed by the famous violinist Isaac Stern. He recommended Ma to Leonard Rose, a teacher at Juilliard School of Music. Ma began to study with Rose.

When Ma was eight, he was asked to play on a national television show. The next year, he made his debut at Carnegie Hall.

From the ages of 9 to 16, Ma studied at Juilliard with Leonard Rose and Janos Scholz. Ma later said that the two men taught him all there was to know about cello playing.

But things did not go so smoothly for Ma during his teenage years. First, there was the problem of living in the middle of two very different worlds. Ma struggled to deal with his Chinese and American cultures.

Ma's Chinese parents were very strict. Ma had to be quiet and submissive. Life was highly structured. Only Chinese was spoken in the home. And Ma was taught Chinese culture and values.

But Ma was not living in China. He was living in New York. He was going to school with American children whose values were very different. American children were allowed to speak up and state their opinions.

Ma couldn't rebel at home. So he began getting into trouble at school. He cut classes and wandered the streets. In 1968, Ma was sent to the Professional Children's School. Teachers there thought he was just bored. So they put him on a faster academic program. Ma ended up graduating from high school at 15.

Ma entered Columbia University. But his personal problems got in the way of his studies. He began drinking and skipping classes. He finally dropped out without even telling his parents.

Finally, Ma realized that another thing was bothering him. His talent made him different from other young people. Some of them teased him. Others thought he was a "freak." All his wild behavior was his way of trying to be more like one of the guys.

Ma got himself back on track. He entered Harvard University. There he studied history and whatever else interested him. Ma later told *The New Yorker*, "I wanted to try and tie together the various threads of my life—my Chinese upbringing, the atmosphere of Paris, my totally different experience in America. Studying history was a way of putting these diverse cultures in perspective."

While studying at Harvard, Ma began getting more and more requests to play concerts. His schedule became unbearably crowded between school and his music. Again, Ma thought about dropping out of Harvard. He knew by then that he could earn a living playing the cello.

Ma's father advised him to stick it out. So, Ma cut back his performances to one a month. And he graduated from Harvard at the age of 21.

In 1977, Ma married Jill Horner, his longtime girlfriend. Ma's father did not approve at first. Jill was an American. But when two grandchildren were later born, Ma's father was won over. But he gave each child a Chinese name!

In 1978, Ma won the Avery Fisher Prize. This is the biggest award in classical music. The winner of the prize gets the chance to perform with major symphony orchestras across the country.

Ma began spending most of his time on the road. At one point, he was giving as many as 150 concerts a season. He was becoming burned out and tired.

When Ma's first child was born in 1983, he knew he needed to slow down and get some balance in his life. His family became his first priority. He began giving fewer performances. But he made sure that every performance, big or small, would be special.

Ma was trained to play classical music. He is widely praised for his performances of Bach, Mozart, and Beethoven. But Ma does not limit his playing to classical works. He also plays a lot of twentieth-century music. In 1992, he recorded a jazz album with singer Bobby McFerrin.

Ma has entered the computer age, too. In 1992, he worked with Todd Machover, a composer at MIT who hooked up a cello to a computer. This setup makes one cello sound like 60. Ma performed Machover's *Begin Again Again,* a work for "hypercello."

Ma is indeed a musical genius. He has made over 50 recordings. He has received eight Grammy awards.

Ma is a musician whose work has been praised since early childhood. But he thinks of himself as just a performing musician. He gives the composers the credit for the beautiful music he plays. Ma thinks of himself as just the vehicle for bringing the music to the audience. His goal in life is to bring exciting, beautiful music to people everywhere.

When Ma is relaxing at home in Boston, he loves to listen to music himself. He listens to all kinds of music. He especially enjoys jazz. But, he doesn't listen to cello music!

Remembering the Facts

1. Why did Yo-Yo Ma come by his musical talent naturally?

2. How did Ma choose the cello?

3. How did Ma's father teach young Ma to play complex musical pieces?

4. At what famous school did Ma study the cello with Leonard Rose from the ages of 9 to 16?

5. Why did Ma find Chinese and American cultures conflicting?

6. Why did Ma study history at Harvard University?

7. What prize did Ma win in 1978?

8. What effect did having a child have on Ma's outlook on life?

9. What is "hypercello"?

10.   Why does Ma give the composer the credit for the beautiful music he plays?

Understanding the Story

11.   Yo-Yo Ma found it difficult living with one set of values at home and another at school. This is a problem many children face. What would be some advice you could give someone in this situation?

12.   In what ways do you think it could be difficult for a teenager to be gifted in some way, as Ma was?

Getting the Main Idea

Why is technical expertise alone not enough to make a good musician?

Applying What You've Learned

Imagine that you have been assigned a long poem to memorize in one week's time. Describe how you would go about this task using the technique that Yo-Yo Ma's father used to teach his young son long musical pieces.

David Ho

Physician and AIDS Researcher

Today, everyone has heard of AIDS. This frightening disease affects huge numbers of people worldwide. Worst of all, there is no known cure for AIDS. It is always fatal. Dr. David Ho has been working with AIDS since before the disease even had a name. Today, he is at the forefront of AIDS research. He directs one of the most important centers in the world for AIDS research.

David Ho

Ho was born in Taiwan in 1952. Taiwan is an island off the coast of mainland China. Taiwan is also known as Formosa or the Republic of China. Taiwan is a Nationalist state, while mainland China is Communist.

Ho's father was an engineer. Young Ho's main hobby as a boy was playing with a chemistry set in the garage.

The family moved from Taiwan to Los Angeles when Ho was 12 years old. At the time, he spoke no English. A year later he was speaking it well.

Ho graduated from high school in Los Angeles. He went on to California Institute of Technology to study physics. He graduated in 1974. After that, Ho went to Harvard Medical School. The program at Harvard strongly emphasized medical research. So, by the time Ho graduated with his medical degree, he had decided to go into research instead of private practice.

While in medical school, Ho married his wife, Susan. The couple later had three children.

After getting his M.D. in 1978, Ho went back to Los Angeles. He did his internship and residency at Cedars-Sinai Medical Center.

In 1981, while working as chief resident, Ho had two patients who would set the course of his future career. These two men both were dying of pneumonia. The strange thing was that the immune systems of both had totally shut down. And there was no apparent cause for their illness.

The two cases were clearly similar. But Ho and the other doctors were puzzled. They couldn't find anything in the scientific literature to explain it. It seemed to be a new disease that wiped out the immune system. From that time on, Ho began to devote most of his time to the study of this new disease.

At the time, there were only two cases of the strange disease known to Ho. But he kept researching it, because he was curious.

Unfortunately, the disease did not remain isolated for long. Soon, more and more people began coming in every week. By mid-1981, it was clear that the disease was spreading rapidly.

By the middle of 1982, AIDS officially got its name. AIDS stands for acquired immune deficiency syndrome. The immune system is the body's disease-fighting system. This system is weakened or destroyed by AIDS.

AIDS is caused by the HIV virus. This virus attacks certain white blood cells called helper T cells. The helper T cells are the body's first line of defense against infections. With these cells destroyed, the person is defenseless against infections of all kinds.

Pneumonia is the infection that most often sets in. Years may go by between a person's infection with HIV and the appearance of AIDS. But when AIDS appears, it is always fatal.

In 1982, Ho returned to Harvard to do more research. His work was done at Massachusetts General Hospital. He began looking for the virus that caused AIDS.

In 1984, Ho and his co-workers were the first to isolate HIV from semen. They also showed that people could be in a "healthy carrier state" of HIV infection. That means that the person is infected with HIV but appears to be healthy.

In 1985, Ho found that HIV is not normally found in saliva. This finding was important because it meant that HIV is not spread from person to person by casual touch, coughs, and so on. Ho's finding helped to calm the public's fears of getting HIV from just being around someone who is infected.

Rather, it was clear by this time that HIV must get into the bloodstream for a person to be infected. Drug users who share hypodermic needles can spread the disease. A person could get a blood transfusion of tainted blood. Usually, however, it is passed by sexual contact with an infected person.

In 1987, Ho returned to UCLA in California. He continued to devote most of his time to AIDS research.

In 1990, the Aaron Diamond AIDS Research Center was being formed in New York City. Ho was asked to be the director of the center. He was given $13 million and told to create a world-class lab, filling it with the best scientists in the world.

At the time, Ho was only 38 years old. It is most unusual for someone so young to be heading a huge research lab. Ho told *New York* magazine, "I've been in AIDS research from the beginning; so in this field, I'm as senior as anyone."

The Diamond Center is one of two major AIDS research centers in the United States. (The other is the Gladstone Institute in San Francisco.) Ho heads a team of about 40 scientists. The Diamond

Center receives half of its money from the federal government. Ho thinks more money should be given to AIDS research. He told *New York* magazine, "There should be a lot more, considering there are . . . 50 million cases worldwide projected in 5 years. It's cheaper to research a cure now than pay for treating all those people later."

Some of the problems Ho and his team are working on now include:

- Exactly how HIV infection develops into AIDS
- How the immune system is affected by HIV
- How HIV is transmitted from a mother to her unborn child
- How HIV is transmitted during sexual contact
- What viral components will be needed for a successful vaccine

Ho and his team are making steady progress in understanding the puzzling disease known as AIDS. But Ho thinks a cure for the disease is not likely to be found soon. He thinks an AIDS vaccine may not be available for another five to ten years.

Ho has earned fame in the medical world for his AIDS research. He has published over 100 scientific journal articles. He has become known by the public as well. Magic Johnson, the famous Los Angeles Laker's basketball star, was ill. Ho had the unhappy task of diagnosing Johnson as HIV positive. Since that time, he has continued to treat the basketball star.

Ho is recognized as a pioneer in the field of AIDS research. Under his direction, the Diamond Center has developed into an outstanding research facility. Perhaps one day, Ho and his research team will discover the cure for AIDS, which is becoming one of the worst epidemics in history.

Remembering the Facts

1. Where was David Ho born?

2. Why did Ho go into medical research instead of private practice?

3. How did Ho become interested in studying AIDS?

4. What is the immune system?

5. How does HIV attack the body?

6. What is meant by the term "healthy carrier state"?

7. What was the importance of Ho's finding that HIV is rarely found in saliva?

8. What AIDS research center does Ho direct?

9. Why does Ho think more money should be given to AIDS research?

10. How did Ho gain fame outside scientific circles?

Understanding the Story

11. Magic Johnson's diagnosis as HIV positive was met with dismay by millions of Americans. By this time, most people were aware of AIDS. Why do you think Johnson's diagnosis was so distressing?

12. Do you think Congress should provide more money for AIDS research? Why or why not?

Getting the Main Idea

Why is Ho's work so important to everyone?

Applying What You've Learned

How do you think teenagers should be best educated to prevent the spread of AIDS? How do you think educational programs could reach people in remote areas of the world?

Wendy Lee Gramm

Economist

Wendy Lee Gramm

Sugar has played a big role in Wendy Lee Gramm's family history. Her grandparents were field hands in the sugarcane fields of Hawaii. Her father worked for the sugar company, too. But he worked his way up through the company, becoming a vice president. Wendy Lee Gramm became an economist. She ended up working with sugar futures in her job as chair of the Commodity Futures Trading Commission.

Wendy Lee was born in 1945 in Waialua, Hawaii. She was the third of four children. Her mother was a librarian. Her father worked for the Waialua Sugar Company.

Wendy's grandparents were from Korea. Both her grandfathers came to Hawaii in search of a better life. In order to pay their way, they signed an agreement with the sugar company. The company would pay their fare. Then they would work in the sugarcane fields until they had paid off their fare. This kind of deal was called "contract labor."

There were few Koreans in Hawaii. So when Wendy's maternal grandfather was ready to marry, he sent back to Korea for a "picture bride."

Very few Asian women came to America at that time. The men were ready to marry. But there were no Asian women. It was against the law for an Asian to marry a white person. So, the men sent back to their native land for picture brides.

The man sent a picture of himself to a matchmaker in Korea. The matchmaker showed the picture to a woman. If she liked the man's looks, she sent him her picture. If he thought she looked suitable, he sent for her. Then they married.

When Wendy Lee was five years old, war broke out in Korea. Communists from North Korea invaded South Korea in 1950. The United States sent troops to help South Korea. Her grandparents went back to South Korea to help, too. Her grandmother worked as a telephone operator. Her grandfather drove a taxi. Both received awards from the South Korean government after the war. They had helped keep South Korea free from communism. They came back to Hawaii to live when the Korean War ended in 1952.

Wendy's father had a degree in engineering. He worked for the same sugar company his parents had worked for. He became the first Asian to be a manager of the company.

The family lived in the country near the sugar company. It was a very relaxed place to live. The children could go barefoot to school until they reached fifth grade.

When Wendy was 12 years old, an event halfway around the world changed her future. The Soviet Union launched the first satellite, *Sputnik*, into space. Americans were upset. The Soviets were ahead of them in the space race.

The race between the two countries became fierce. American education began stressing science and math. Wendy became interested in math. She worked hard and took advanced courses in math.

After high school, she went to Wellesley College as a math major. She found math in college boring. She decided to switch her major to economics. That way, she would still be using her math background.

She graduated from college in 1966. She continued her education at Northwestern University in Illinois. There she completed a Ph.D. in economics in 1971.

Wendy Lee interviewed for a teaching job at Texas A & M University. Present at the interview was Philip Gramm. He was a professor at the school. The interview was a success in two ways. She got the job. And she met her future husband. She and Gramm were married three months later.

Now, both of them were teaching at Texas A & M. And in just a few years, they had two sons.

Phil Gramm was interested in politics. In 1976, he ran for the Senate as a Democrat and lost. Two years later, he ran for House of Representatives and won. Two months later, the Gramm family moved to Washington, D.C.

Wendy Gramm's first job in Washington, D.C., was with the Institute for Defense Analysis. Then, in 1982, she began working for the Federal Trade Commission (FTC). She found she enjoyed this work.

In the meantime, her husband had been reelected to the House in 1980 and 1982 as a Democrat. Then, in 1983, he decided to become a Republican. In 1984, he ran for the U.S. Senate as a

Republican. Wendy Gramm resigned her job with the FTC to help him campaign. He won the race. He became a United States Senator from Texas.

In 1985, Wendy Gramm took a new job. She began working for the Office of Management and Budget (OMB). One of her jobs there was to try to limit the number of regulations made by the government—a real challenge.

In 1987, President Reagan chose her to head the Commodity Futures Trading Commission (CFTC). The president's nomination of the CFTC chair required the approval of the U.S. Senate's Agriculture Committee. Gramm appeared before the committee and answered many questions.

She brought with her two witnesses who spoke in her favor. One of these was Senator Daniel K. Inouye (see pages 1–5). He praised Gramm for her many fine qualities. The second witness was Senator Lloyd Bentsen of Texas, who spoke in her favor.

Gramm was approved by the Senate. She was sworn in as chair of the CFTC on February 22, 1988. She was approved for a second term as chair in 1990.

The CFTC is responsible for overseeing the trading of commodities. Commodities are products like sugar, wheat, cattle, and gold. There are over 400 commodity brokerage firms. Fifty-five thousand commodity sellers and 7500 floor brokers come under the CFTC's rule.

The CFTC makes sure commodity markets are run honestly. It also protects market customers.

The CFTC regulates commodity futures and options trading. A futures contract is a promise to buy or sell a commodity at a specific price on a certain date. Futures options give the right to buy or sell futures contracts if desired. The CFTC licenses futures exchanges where futures contracts may be bought or sold.

When President Bill Clinton took office in 1993, Gramm resigned her position. She would be replaced with a Democrat.

Shortly after that, she became a board member of the Chicago Mercantile Exchange, a large commodity trading exchange. She is also a board member of the Enron Corporation. Gramm has many accomplishments in academics, government, and private industry.

Remembering the Facts

1. What is contract labor?

2. Why did so many Asian Americans working in America send back to their native land for picture brides?

3. Why did Wendy Lee's grandparents return to South Korea between 1950 and 1952?

4. Why was it unusual for Gramm's father to have a managerial position in the sugar company?

5. What effect did the launching of *Sputnik* have on American education?

6. Where did Gramm get her first teaching job?

7. Why did the Gramm family move to Washington, D.C.?

8. What position did President Reagan appoint Gramm to in 1987?

9. What is a futures contract?

10. Why did Gramm resign her position in 1993?

Understanding the Story

11. When Wendy Gramm took the job as chair of the CFTC, some people thought she was hired because she was Phil Gramm's wife. Their complaints did not last long. Gramm soon proved she knew what she was doing. How do you think being married to a senator could affect her career? What might be the pros and cons?

12. What would be the pros and cons of a presidential candidate being married to an Asian American? How might voters view such a marriage?

Getting the Main Idea

Why do you think Wendy Lee Gramm has been an asset to the Asian-American community?

Applying What You've Learned

Gramm gives her parents and grandparents the credit for teaching her to work hard and stick to her values. Write a paragraph telling how you learned some of your values from another person's good example.

Ellison Onizuka

Astronaut

Ellison Onizuka's grandparents came to Hawaii from Japan. They worked as field hands on a sugar plantation. They had come to America in the hopes of finding a better life. But never in their wildest dreams did they think that one day their grandson would soar above the clouds in a spacecraft.

Onizuka was born in 1946 in the village of Kealakekua, Hawaii. He was the third of four children. His parents ran a small general store.

Onizuka had a lot of energy as a boy. He loved to climb and explore the island. He

Ellison Onizuka

also liked to take things apart to see how they worked. The problem was that he wasn't always able to put them back together.

Onizuka's family tried to help him channel his energy into worthwhile things. He worked hard in school. He played baseball and basketball. And he especially loved Boy Scouting. He reached the rank of Eagle Scout as a senior in high school.

The area where Onizuka lived raised some of the best coffee in the world: Kona coffee. Schools closed from August to November so children could help harvest the beans. Onizuka worked in the fields each year.

From a young age, Onizuka was interested in space. He loved going to Honolulu's Bishop Museum, where he could look through a telescope at the stars. As a teenager, Onizuka followed Walter Schirra's work on the *Mercury* space program. He did some experiments of his own, too. One day he set off a Roman candle under his family's house to see what would happen.

Onizuka's parents didn't know what to think about their son's dreams of space. His mother later told *Time* magazine, "Ellison always had it in his mind to become an astronaut. But he was too embarrassed to tell anyone. When he was growing up, there were no Asian astronauts, no black astronauts, just white ones. His dream seemed too big."

In 1964, Onizuka graduated from high school. He went to Boulder, Colorado, to study aerospace engineering at the University of Colorado. It was a big change from the warm, sunny climate of Hawaii to the cold mountains of Colorado. Onizuka took up snow skiing. He found it harder than riding sand-sliding boards on the beaches of Hawaii.

Onizuka did well in his studies. In 1969, he earned a master of science degree in aerospace engineering. That same year, he married Lorna Yoshida, a fellow Hawaiian. They later had two daughters.

In 1970, Onizuka joined the U.S. Air Force. For the next four years, he worked at McClellan Air Force Base near Sacramento, California. There he worked on flight test programs and flight safety systems.

Onizuka applied for the Air Force Test Pilot School. He was accepted in 1974. He moved to Edwards Air Force Base. His job was to go with test pilots and make sure new aircraft systems were working correctly. He also learned to fly some 43 different kinds of planes.

Four years later, Onizuka was one of 35 people chosen by NASA to be trained as astronauts. He moved to Johnson Space Center in Houston. In 1979, Onizuka completed the training program. Now he was eligible to be assigned as a mission specialist on space shuttle flights.

Finally, Onizuka got his turn to fly. In 1982, he was chosen to be a crew member on a secret space shuttle mission. The mission was postponed again and again. Finally, on January 24, 1985, *Discovery* soared into space. The shuttle completed 48 orbits of Earth. It landed safely at Kennedy Space Center in Florida after three days in space.

On the flight, Onizuka took special mementos: Kona coffee, macadamia nuts, a Buddhist medallion from his father, and patches from the Japanese-American 442nd Combat Team. (See the story on Daniel Inouye, pages 1–5.)

Onizuka, now a lieutenant colonel, had become the first Asian American in space. He was also the first Hawaiian and the first Buddhist in space. To all these groups, he was a hero. For months after the flight, he gave speeches about his experience. He gave most of his talks to schoolchildren.

In one of these speeches, he talked about his thoughts during the spaceflight: "I looked down as we passed over Hawaii and thought about all the sacrifices of all the people who helped me along the way. My grandparents, who were contract laborers; my parents, who did without to send me to college; my schoolteachers, coaches, and ministers—all the past generations who pulled together to create the present. Different people, different races, different religions—all working toward a common goal, all one family." (as quoted in *The Japanese Americans*)

Later in 1985, Onizuka was chosen to fly a mission aboard *Challenger.* This flight was not to be a secret military mission. It included a mix of military and nonmilitary people.

On January 28, 1986, the crew boarded *Challenger* with great excitement. Thousands of people had come to Kennedy Space Center in Florida to see the liftoff. Millions more watched on television.

At 11:38 A.M., the ground shook as the shuttle engines roared to life. In just seconds, *Challenger* cleared the launch tower. The audience followed the shuttle's progress into the clear blue sky. The twenty-fifth space shuttle flight seemed to be well under way.

But 73 seconds after liftoff, the nightmare began. Unknown to the astronauts or the ground crew, a jet of flame was beginning to lick around the giant fuel tank. It was coming from a malfunctioning booster rocket. Seconds later, there was a terrible explosion. The fuel tank was ripped open from nose to tail. All seven crew members died instantly.

The entire country was struck with grief. It was the first time any American astronaut had been lost during a mission. It was the worst disaster in almost 25 years of manned spaceflight.

President Reagan came on television to honor the astronauts. "The crew of the space shuttle *Challenger* honored us by the manner in which they lived their lives. We will never forget them, not the last time we saw them, this morning, as they prepared for their journey and waved goodbye, and 'slipped the surly bonds of Earth to touch the face of God.'"

Indeed, astronaut Onizuka will not soon be forgotten by his loved ones or by the many schoolchildren whose lives he touched. Some of his outlook on life can be seen in this part of the speech he gave at the 1980 graduation of Konawaena High School:

"If I can impress on you only one idea tonight, let it be that the people who make this world run, whose lives can be termed successful, whose names will go down in the history books are not the cynics, the critics, or the armchair quarterbacks.

"They are the adventurers, the explorers, and doers of this world. When they see a wrong or a problem, they do something about it. When they see a vacant place in our knowledge, they work to fill that void.

"Rather than leaning back and criticizing how things are, they work to make things the way they should be. . . . Make your life count—and the world will be a better place because you tried."

In 1991, the Ellison S. Onizuka Space Center opened at the Keahole Airport in Kona, Hawaii. This $2 million museum was built not far from the coffee fields where young Onizuka used to daydream about flying among the stars. Onizuka has a memorial in space, too. An asteroid was named for him.

Remembering the Facts

1. What work did Onizuka's grandparents do when they came to Hawaii?

2. What rank did Onizuka achieve in scouting?

3. Why did the schools Onizuka attended in Hawaii close from August to November?

4. Why didn't Onizuka's parents know what to think about his dream to be an astronaut?

5. What subject did Onizuka study at the University of Colorado?

6. What job did Onizuka do with the test pilots at the Air Force Test Pilot School?

7. What three "firsts" did Onizuka achieve when he went on the *Discovery* mission?

8.   Name two of the mementos Onizuka took on his flight.

9.   What caused the explosion on *Challenger*?

10.   What museum was built in Hawaii to honor Onizuka?

Understanding the Story

11.   NASA chose only 35 people to train as astronauts out of 8100 candidates. Onizuka was chosen because of his engineering background, his physical condition, and his friendly personality. Why do you think personality would enter into NASA's selection of astronauts?

12.   Why do you think that the men of the Japanese-American 442nd Combat Team were heroes to Ellison Onizuka?

Getting the Main Idea

Neil Armstrong, the first man to walk on the moon, said of Onizuka, "Ellison Onizuka had his life cut short for reasons he could not control. Yet during his years, he accomplished much more than most. Our world is a better place for his being here. . . ." What do you think was Onizuka's most important accomplishment?

Applying What You've Learned

Onizuka once told *The New York Times* that during liftoff ". . . you're aware that you're on top of a monster, you're totally at the mercy of the vehicle." Imagine you are an astronaut aboard the space shuttle *Discovery*. Write a paragraph describing your feelings before, during, and after liftoff.

Carlos Bulosan

Poet and Writer

Carlos Bulosan was born in Binalonan, in the Philippines. The date of his birth is not known. But it was sometime between 1911 and 1914.

Bulosan's parents were peasants. They worked hard to support their large family by farming four acres of land. Bulosan helped his father in the fields. He went with his mother as she walked from village to village selling salt fish.

Bulosan's parents could not read or write. But they sensed the value of education. The boy was allowed to go to

Carlos Bulosan

the village school for three years. After that, it was necessary for him to begin working full-time.

Bulosan's parents picked one of their other sons, Marcario, to go on to high school, to become a teacher. The school was in another town. So students had to pay for their room and board.

To pay for this huge expense, Bulosan's parents mortgaged their farm. They hoped that their son would later earn enough from his teaching to pay off the debt. Marcario graduated and began teaching. But his earnings were never enough to pay off the whole debt in time. Eventually the farm was lost.

The family had no hope of escaping their poverty. So, Carlos Bulosan left Binalonan and his childhood at the age of 13. He hoped to make his own way.

Bulosan went to the nearby city of Baguio. There he found a job as a houseboy for an American artist named Mary Strandon. Strandon had come to the Philippines to paint. She supported herself by working in the local library.

While working for Strandon, Bulosan began learning English. Strandon gave him books from the library to read. Soon he began working in the library. A whole new world began to open up for the poor boy who had grown up in a grass hut.

As Bulosan said in his autobiography, "I was beginning to understand what was going on around me. The darkness that had covered my present life was lifting. I was emerging into the sunlight . . . ." It was at this time that Bulosan decided to go to America.

It took him two years to save enough money for passage on a ship bound for Seattle. Bulosan thought his troubles would be over if he could reach the shining land of America.

The voyage to America was not easy. All the Filipino passengers were kept belowdecks at all times. In this dark hole, Bulosan lay on his bunk for days. He was without food, seasick, and lonely. He wondered how he would survive in America.

In fact, he was lucky to survive the voyage at all. During the trip, an epidemic of meningitis broke out. Most of the Filipinos became ill. Many died.

In June 1930, Bulosan arrived in Seattle. He had not picked a good time to come to America. It was the depth of the Great Depression. All over the country, people were out of work. Competition was fierce for any available jobs. So it wasn't surprising that Americans resented the newly arrived immigrants.

Bulosan and a few friends found a cheap hotel room. But they were robbed. Then, they could not pay for their room. To get his money, the hotel owner sold Bulosan for $5 to a man seeking workers for a fish cannery in Alaska.

So, after only one day in America, Bulosan found himself on the way to Alaska. He did three months of hard labor there. At the end of the season, he was paid $13. The rest of his earnings were kept by the cannery owners, "for expenses."

Bulosan's next job was even worse. He was paid nothing for months of apple picking in Washington state. Angry white men burned the Filipino workers' bunkhouse and chased them away. Bulosan was forced to flee for his life. He and others rode empty boxcars to California. Along the way, he worked picking crops when he could.

In California, there was little work. But worse, the Filipinos were the targets of constant racial violence. Cars with Filipino men were often targets. Their cars were stopped by the police and searched. Filipinos were beaten or shot for little or no reason. Bulosan wrote in his autobiography, "I came to know that, in many ways, it was a crime to be a Filipino in California. I came to know that the public streets were not free to my people."

Bulosan became involved in efforts to improve things for Filipinos. From 1935 to 1941, he worked to help organize migrant workers into labor unions. Because of this work, Bulosan was beaten and driven out of town after town.

Bulosan had begun writing at this time. In 1934, he began writing for *The New Tide.* This was a Filipino literary magazine. He also began writing poetry, short stories, and articles.

Then, in 1936, Bulosan came down with tuberculosis. It took him two years in the hospital to recover. For the first time in his life, he had the time and opportunity to read all he wanted.

He spent long hours reading and writing. He wrote in his autobiography, "I locked myself in the room, pulled down the shades, and shut out the whole world. I knew enough of it to carry me for a lifetime of writing."

Finally, conditions in the United States began to improve. The Depression ended. World War II began, with the United States and the Philippines fighting as allies. Much of the terrible prejudice and hatred against Filipinos began to lessen.

During this time, Bulosan's work began to gain notice. In 1942, he published his first two books of poems, *Letter from America* and *Chorus for America.* The next year, he published *The Voice of Bataan.* This book honored the soldiers, Filipino and American, who died in the battle of Bataan.

Bulosan's work was published widely in a number of magazines. *The Laughter of My Father* (1944) was a collection of these stories.

In 1946, Bulosan published his autobiography, *America Is in the Heart.* The book became an instant best-seller. In this book, he tells of his years of struggle, abuse, and illness. He tells of his work to unite Filipinos in America. Finally, he tells how the power of his pen allowed him to reach his goals. Through all these struggles, Bulosan never lost faith in America.

In *America Is in the Heart*, he wrote, "America is not a land of one race or one class of men. We are all Americans [who] have toiled and suffered and known oppression and defeat, from the first Indian that offered peace in Manhattan to the last Filipino pea pickers. America is not merely a land. America is in the hearts of men that died for freedom; it is also in the eyes of men that are building a new world. . . . All of us, from the first Adams to the last Filipino, native-born or alien, educated or illiterate—*we are America!*"

In the early 1950's, Bulosan's health began to weaken. In 1956, he died of tuberculosis and malnutrition.

After his death, Bulosan's writings were largely forgotten. But in the 1970's, a new generation of Asian Americans discovered his work. *America Is in the Heart* was reprinted in 1973. It has become a classic in the field of Asian-American studies.

Remembering the Facts

1. How did the Bulosan family lose their farm?

2. Why did Bulosan leave home at age 13?

3. How did Bulosan learn English?

4. Why did Bulosan decide to go to America?

5. Why did Americans resent the newly arrived Filipinos?

6. What happened to Bulosan after only one day in America?

7. How did Bulosan work to improve the lot of his fellow Filipinos?

8. What is the name of Bulosan's autobiography?

9. What is one of the themes of his autobiography?

10. Why was Bulosan's work rediscovered in the 1970's?

Understanding the Story

11. Carlos Bulosan overcame poverty, illiteracy, and prejudice to become a powerful writer. What do you think was the most important thing he did that allowed him to develop this skill?

12.   What do you think the title of Bulosan's autobiography, *America Is in the Heart*, means?

Getting the Main Idea

Why do you think *America Is in the Heart* is a basic text in Asian-American studies courses across the country?

Applying What You've Learned

Filipinos in the 1930's were subjected to violent racism. Do you think racism is a problem where you live? Why or why not? If it is a problem, tell ways you think race relations could be improved.

Jose Aruego

Illustrator

Jose Aruego was born in 1932 in Manila, the capital of the Philippines. From the time he was a boy, he knew he was supposed to be a lawyer.

After all, law ran in his family. Aruego's father was a law professor at the University of Manila. He was also active in politics. Aruego's sister was a lawyer. And most of his friends were lawyers.

Aruego had no interest in studying law. But he did what was expected of him. He went to law school. In 1955, he earned his law degree from the University of the Philippines.

Jose Aruego

Aruego's law career lasted for three months. After losing his very first case, he decided he had made a big mistake. Not only that, he decided it wasn't too late to change his mind. He knew what he really wanted to do.

Aruego had always loved two things: comic books and animals. He had a big collection of comic books. He also collected pets. At one time he had "three horses, seven dogs and their puppies, half-a-dozen cats and their kittens, a yard full of chickens, roosters, and pigeons, a pond full of frogs, tadpoles, and ducks, and three fat pigs."

Jose Aruego's dream was to draw comic books or cartoons. He especially loved drawing funny animals doing funny things. So, he left his law career. He started all over.

Aruego went to New York City. There he studied at the Parsons School of Design. He missed his friends and family terribly. But he was finally doing what he loved. In 1959, he received a certificate in graphic arts and advertising.

His first job as an artist was at a Greenwich Village studio. His task was to glue feathers on the wings of Christmas angel mannequins. That job lasted only as long as the Christmas season.

For the next six years, Aruego worked for a variety of ad agencies, design studios, and magazines. In 1961, he married Ariane Dewey, who was also an artist. They had one son, Juan.

During this time, Aruego also drew cartoons. Each week he drew about 20 of them. Then he tried to sell them to magazine cartoon editors. Sometimes, editors choose to publish one. But some weeks none of the cartoons sold. Aruego was paid for each cartoon that made it into a magazine.

He began selling his cartoons to *Look*, *Saturday Evening Post*, and *The New Yorker*. It was not a steady income by any means. But Aruego quit his advertising jobs to have more time to spend on cartooning.

Aruego decided to try his hand at doing a children's book. He wrote and illustrated a book called *The King and His Friends*. It is never easy to get a first book published. But Aruego was lucky to find an editor who liked his cartoonlike drawings. The book was published in 1969. Aruego dedicated the book to his son, Juan.

The King and His Friends was not a best-seller. But it did well enough to earn Aruego attention. He soon landed jobs illustrating books for other authors.

In 1970, he illustrated a book for author Robert Kraus. It was called *Whose Mouse Are You?* The book was honored as an American Library Association Notable Book Selection. After that, Aruego was in demand.

In 1970, he wrote *Juan and the Asuangs.* This book won a *New York Times* award as an outstanding picture book of the year. Over the years, Aruego has won many other awards for his work.

In 1973, Aruego and his wife divorced. But they continued working together on many books. One of their most popular is *We Hide, You Seek.* This book was written in 1979 and is still in print today.

We Hide, You Seek took eight years to complete. Yet it has a text of only 27 words. This book has been widely praised by critics. And it is loved by children.

The story is about a clumsy rhinoceros playing a game of hide-and-seek with his African animal friends. The lesson the book teaches is about camouflage.

One scene shows the animals hiding in various places in the jungle. By looking carefully, children can find them. The next scene shows the clumsy rhino entering the picture. Accidentally, he uncovers the animals and they run away.

Another book that is typical of Aruego's work is *Look What I Can Do.* This book has only 20 words. But the antics of the funny animals in the illustrations expand the text.

Aruego has written and illustrated more than 50 children's books. He is best known for his drawings of funny animals. He does not like to do serious drawings.

Sometimes Aruego writes a story and illustrates it. His books usually have a simple text. Then he uses humorous pictures to enrich the text of his picture books.

Aruego knows that children like to laugh and have fun. So, he tries to make the drawings in his books fun to look at. His most important goal in all his work is to appeal to children. He believes that his funny animals are easy for children to identify with and to love.

His illustrations begin with simple, yet detailed, line drawings. He is also a master of the use of color. In fact, many critics note that Aruego's works do not really need words at all to tell their story.

Aruego also illustrates books for other authors. In this case, he works with an editor to illustrate a story another person has written. The author and illustrator do not usually talk about the story. The editor works as a go-between.

Two of Aruego's own favorite books are ones he did nearly 25 years ago. They are *Whose Mouse Are You?* (1970) and *Leo the Late Bloomer* (1971). He illustrated both of these books for writer Robert Kraus. Both still sell very well.

Today, Aruego continues to write and illustrate children's books. He is pleased that his childhood loves—drawing and animals—have made up his adult career. It is clear that he loves his work. And children love the work he has done.

Remembering the Facts

1. Where was Jose Aruego born?

2. What profession did Aruego's father want him to follow?

3. Why did Aruego change careers?

4. What were Aruego's two loves as a child?

5. Why did Aruego decide to go to New York City?

6. Why was it difficult to make a living drawing cartoons?

7. How did Aruego get started illustrating children's books?

8. What is the subject of most of Aruego's drawings?

9. What is Aruego's goal in all his work?

10. Name one of Aruego's two favorites of his own work.

Understanding the Story

11. Why do you think Jose Aruego went to law school when he had no interest in law as a career?

12. Although Aruego has written and illustrated over 50 children's books, he says that he is still learning his craft. He told someone at Greenwillow Books that "Each project teaches me something new. . . ." What do you think this says about Aruego's attitude toward his work?

Getting the Main Idea

Jose Aruego had the courage to leave a career he did not like and start over in an area that he loved. Why do you think it is important to choose work you both enjoy and can do well?

Applying What You've Learned

Art critics say that Aruego's illustrations can stand alone to tell a story without words. Think of a simple story line. Tell your story by drawing a series of pictures, similar to a comic strip. Use no words in your story.

Dustin Nguyen

Activist Actor

Dustin Nguyen was born in 1962 in Saigon, the capital of South Vietnam. His real name is Nguyen Xuan Tri.

Nguyen's father was a well-known television producer. His mother was an actress and dancer. The family lived well in a beautiful custom-built home designed by Nguyen's father and cared for by servants.

Nguyen was a good student. When he finished sixth grade, he took a two-day exam to get into a top high school. Only a small percentage of

Dustin Nguyen

those applying were admitted. Nguyen scored in the top 5 percent of those taking the test.

The school was very strict. Students had to wear uniforms. Students who did not behave were hit with a ruler. There were very few discipline problems in the school.

Nguyen's childhood was sheltered and pampered. But all around him trouble was brewing. Nguyen's world was about to fall apart.

In 1954, the Geneva Convention had divided Vietnam into two parts at the 17th parallel. The Communists controlled North Vietnam and the Nationalists got South Vietnam.

The two Vietnams were engaged in a civil war. The Communist soldiers were called the Vietcong. They were trained by the North Vietnamese and backed by the Chinese.

The Vietcong were experts in guerrilla warfare. By 1961, South Vietnam was in trouble. The United States began sending military equipment and money. President Lyndon B. Johnson sent U.S. ground troops to Vietnam in 1965. By the end of 1965, there were 184,000 U.S. troops in Vietnam.

The war continued to escalate. By 1968, 550,000 American soldiers had been sent to Vietnam. The annual cost to the United States was over $30 billion. It had become America's war. But with all this, America could not seem to defeat the Vietcong. By 1968, the war had become the longest and most unpopular in American history.

The war dragged on. Finally, in 1973, the United States withdrew its troops, leaving the Vietnamese to fight their own war. The United States continued, however, to send tanks, aircraft, and guns.

In April 1975, when Dustin Nguyen was 12 years old, the Vietcong began a strong drive southward. South Vietnam was overrun, and Saigon fell to the enemy.

The Nguyen family was in grave danger. Nguyen's father had written propaganda urging North Vietnamese people to defect to the South. If he were caught by the North Vietnamese troops, he would be executed.

Thousands of other people had supported the U.S. presence in the war. Now they were all frantic to leave the country. They feared a bloodbath by the Communists. American ships and helicopters evacuated 140,000 South Vietnamese.

The Nguyens left everything they had behind. They rushed to the beach of Vung Tao, where an American cargo ship was approaching the shore to pick up refugees. Nguyen got separated from his family. But he found his best friend, who was also trying to escape. The two boys ran toward the ship.

Just then Vietcong soldiers appeared. They began firing on the fleeing people. Nguyen ran out into the ocean. He turned around just in time to see his best friend shot down in a hail of bullets. There was nothing he could do to help.

Nguyen made it to the rescue ship. There he was reunited with his family. But he will never forget the horror of his escape from Vietnam.

President Gerald Ford admitted the refugees to the United States. The Nguyen family was taken to Fort Chaffee, Arkansas. Here, the government had set up a refugee camp to help the people adjust to life in the United States. The family stayed there three months.

The Methodist Church agreed to sponsor the Nguyen family. They moved into the home of a Kirkwood, Missouri, woman. People there helped the family get clothing and jobs. Nguyen's father began working as a dishwasher and janitor. His mother got a job as a cleaning lady.

A year later, the family was able to buy a small home in Kirkwood. They began to learn English. And Nguyen began going to school.

The Nguyens were the first Vietnamese family in the area. They were not easily accepted. Many Americans had lost friends or relatives in the war. So they were not happy to have Vietnamese people move into their town.

Nguyen entered the eighth grade. He found it hard to make friends. Many of the students teased or ignored him. Then, at the age of 14, he began to study the martial arts. He especially liked Tae Kwon Do. By the time he was 17, he had earned his black belt. He found that this skill gave him self-confidence. Now he knew he could do well at other things, too.

After high school graduation, Nguyen went to Orange Coast College in California. His parents wanted him to become an engineer. But Nguyen had other ideas. He wanted to become an actor.

His parents did not approve of his decision. They were angry and disappointed when he quit college to become an actor. Finally, they worked through it as a family. This was very hard on Nguyen. It was the first time he had ever done anything against his parents' wishes. His parents have since become very proud of him and his accomplishments.

Nguyen moved to Hollywood. He changed his name and became an American citizen. For a year, he tried to get acting jobs. But he did not have much luck.

Nguyen's first role was in the television show *Magnum, P.I.* He played a Cambodian anti-Communist in this 1984 show. In 1985, he appeared for seven months in the soap opera *General Hospital.*

In 1986, he landed a role in *21 Jump Street.* He played the role of Harry Ioki, a young undercover police officer, until 1990.

Nguyen hopes that he is a good representative of the Vietnamese people. He does volunteer work in the fight against drugs and gangs.

He wants to be a role model for young Asian Americans. To this end, he has become involved in DARE (Drug Abuse Resistance Education). This national program teaches children why they should say no to drugs. Nguyen believes that if people can be educated to stay away from drugs, the problem can be eliminated.

He also works to break up problem gangs, especially Asian-American gangs.

Nguyen is still a young man in his thirties. He hopes to do more acting and maybe get into directing and producing shows.

Remembering the Facts

1. Why were there two Vietnams?

2. How were the governments of North and South Vietnam different?

3. Who were the Vietcong?

4. Which president sent U.S. troops to aid South Vietnam in 1965?

5. In what year did the United States withdraw its troops from Vietnam?

6. Why did the Nguyens leave Vietnam?

7. Why did the Nguyens go to Fort Chaffee, Arkansas?

8. What skill did Nguyen learn as a teenager that helped him gain self-confidence?

9. In what television show did Nguyen play the part of Harry Ioki from 1986 to 1990?

10. In what two areas does Nguyen do volunteer work?

Understanding the Story

11. Dustin Nguyen had a hard time being accepted by the other students at his high school. Why do you think so many Americans resented the Vietnamese families who sought refuge in the United States?

12. How do you think Nguyen's escape from Vietnam might affect his outlook on life?

Getting the Main Idea

Why do you think Dustin Nguyen is a good role model for young Asian Americans?

Applying What You've Learned

Imagine that you are a refugee from a war-torn country. You are allowed to enter another country and plan to live the rest of your life there. What do you think would be the hardest adjustments you would have to make? Write a paragraph to explain your answer.

Key Vocabulary

Daniel K. Inouye

nisei	politics	discrimination
ghetto	territory	negotiator
pidgin	legislature	Appropriations
premedical	civil rights	

Maxine Hong Kingston

contributions	culture	ancestors
scholar	scholarship	status
idle	protesting	rejection
midwifery	oppressed	

I.M. Pei

architect	Communists	annex
inscribe	distasteful	acclaim
Buddhist	pueblo	pyramid
invaded	publicity	inventive

Maya Lin

controversial	ceramist	prejudice
Vietnam	site	anonymous
veterans	granite	compromise
shrine	slurs	fiber-optic
monument		

An Wang

Confucius	scrounge	word processing
philosopher	binary	menus
moderation	staple	endowed
simplicity	calculator	outpatient clinic
transmitters	exponential values	

Haing Ngor

guerilla	Communists	latrine
ransom	royalists	refuge
obstetrics	coup	correspondent
gynecology	Khmer Rouge	

Seiji Ozawa

conductor	pacificist	scheme
symphony	deported	commemorating
occupied	endure	universal

Kristi Yamaguchi

technician	corrective	triple axel
internment camps	compulsory	flawless
competing	expertise	endorse
clubfeet	commute	

Noriyuki "Pat" Morita

karate	sabotage	uninsured
migrant	invalid	abundance
spinal tuberculosis	precaution	ethic
relocated	default	persistence
racial discrimination		

Yo-Yo Ma

cellist	suite (of music)	perspective
mainland China	recital	classical music
analyze	debut	priority
viola	submissive	composer
measure of music		

David Ho

AIDS	immune system	saliva
emphasized	HIV	hypodermic
internship	virus	transfusion
residency	helper T cells	tainted
pneumonia	semen	

Wendy Lee Gramm

economist	*Sputnik*	futures
contract labor	space race	options
picture bride	regulation	futures contract
matchmaker	commodity	futures exchange
Korean War		

Ellison Onizuka

aerospace engineering	mission specialist	malfunction
test pilot	memento	booster rocket
	medallion	asteroid

Carlos Bulosan

peasant	Great Depression	tuberculosis
mortgage	competition	allies
belowdecks	racial violence	malnutrition
meningitis	autobiography	

Jose Aruego

graphic arts	illustrate	illustrations
mannequin	camouflage	expand
editor	antics	humorous

Dustin Nguyen

17th parallel	propaganda	evacuated
Vietcong	defect	refugee
guerilla	executed	sponsor
escalate	frantic	martial arts

Answers

DANIEL K. INOUYE

Remembering the Facts

1. Children born in America to parents who came to America from Japan

2. They had to pass the English Standard test to gain entrance to the English Standard schools attended by white children.

3. He studied books on medicine, took a first-aid course, taught first aid, and enrolled in premed at the University of Hawaii.

4. Pearl Harbor was bombed.

5. *(any two)* It was all volunteer, all nisei, and the most decorated army unit in U.S. history.

6. He lost one arm during the war, so he could no longer be a surgeon.

7. He became Hawaii's first representative in the U.S. Congress and the first Japanese American in the U.S. Congress.

8. The Watergate hearings, the Iran-Contra hearings

Understanding the Story

Answers will vary:

9. Japanese Americans looked the same as the people we were at war with. People were afraid they might be spies or secretly loyal to Japan. They feared being harmed. This fear could have been avoided if white Americans had known individual Japanese Americans well and trusted them.

10. Children learn to speak by what they hear around them. For children who grow up hearing standard speech patterns, stan-

dard speech comes easily. For those who grow up hearing nonstandard grammar or a mixture of languages, it is very difficult to learn to speak standard English.

Getting the Main Idea

The story of Daniel K. Inouye shows one man's determination to overcome poverty and discrimination to achieve success. In the words of Hubert Humphrey: "It is the story that reveals the spirit and heart of America. It is the story of a man who worked and studied and fought hard to make his dream come true." It also shows the story of Japanese Americans during the tumultuous World War II period.

Applying What You've Learned

Discrimination can be overcome by hard work and determination to succeed. All people should be treated equally.

MAXINE HONG KINGSTON

Remembering the Facts

1. He could not find a job as a teacher or a poet.
2. 15 years
3. She went to school to learn medicine and midwifery and then became a very successful healer.
4. She was named after a blond gambler who was very lucky.
5. A form of storytelling that combines family stories with myths, legends, and Chinese history
6. From the talk stories of her mother and the other Chinese people who gathered at the laundry
7. She did not speak English and was very shy.
8. It tells of her childhood as a Chinese-American girl.
9. It tells the story of the men in her family.

Understanding the Story

Answers will vary:

10. A child who heard over and over that she was worthless would soon come to believe that. (Girls in China were taught that their lives had little value. They grew up to be submissive and subservient. Maxine Hong Kingston reveals her struggle to overcome this in her book *The Woman Warrior*.)

11. She wrote about discrimination against Chinese Americans and against women. Her writings are distinctly feminist. But they also assert the right of all Chinese Americans to be full-status citizens of the United States.

Getting the Main Idea

A writer's words can be a powerful tool. By bringing discrimination and rejection to the public's attention, Maxine Hong Kingston has gone a long way toward eliminating the problem. In addition, her descriptions of Chinese culture and beliefs create a basis for understanding Chinese ways.

Applying What You've Learned

Answers will vary.

I.M. PEI

Remembering the Facts

1. He lived in Shanghai, where there were many new buildings going up.

2. Many upper-class families sent their children abroad to study. Pei wanted to study architecture in America.

3. The Japanese had invaded China; World War II had begun.

4. Thinking of more efficient ways to blow up enemy buildings

5. China was taken over by the Communists.

6. He rebuilt areas where slums had been cleared.

7. John Hancock Building in Boston
8. *(any three)* National Center for Atmospheric Research; John F. Kennedy Library; East Building annex to the National Gallery of Art; hotel in Beijing; office building for Bank of China; Louvre addition

Understanding the Story

Answers will vary:

9. If an artist does work that is unlike what people are used to seeing, many people will not like it at first. (Pei's work is strikingly original, making use of a lot of geometric shapes and bold forms.)
10. Most architects or artists develop a style that is their own. They are influenced by other architects or artists they study and by things in their own background. This style then shows in all their work.

Getting the Main Idea

His approach to architecture is unique. He has completed a large number of successful structures, each of them creative and unusual. His buildings are really works of art.

Applying What You've Learned

Answers will vary.

MAYA LIN

Remembering the Facts

1. Sculpture and architecture
2. It was an assignment for a class.
3. Two long black granite walls that came together to form a V.
4. Some people wanted a more traditional statue. Others did not like the fact that she was Chinese American.

5. A traditional statue was to be added near the entrance to the memorial site.

6. Those who saw it felt its power as a place of healing.

7. To honor those who had died in the civil rights struggle.

8. In Dr. Martin Luther King, Jr.'s "I have a dream" speech, which included the words "justice rolls down like waters. . . ." The idea of rolling water inspired Maya Lin.

9. For nearly 200 years, no women were allowed into Yale at all.

Understanding the Story

Answers will vary:

10. The wall creates the peaceful feeling of a row of headstones in a grassy cemetery. The names of those who died are engraved on the wall, as they would be on headstones. Those who have lost loved ones can read the names. The memorial seems to help the grieving ones with the process of mourning. They leave flowers and other mementos at the wall, as they would in a cemetery. (So many people have touched the wall or made rubbings of the names of their loved ones that by 1994, it was necessary to do repairs in some areas.)

    It is a permanent tribute to those who have died. It gives a serene, peaceful feeling to those who see it. As Lin describes her work: "This was to say they have died, and we are here among the living. It's not clear-cut because we can see the earth and sky reflected in the names. But it is to make the people walk back into the light. . . . As we turn to leave, we see these walls stretching into the distance, directing us to the Washington Monument to the left, and the Lincoln Memorial to the right, thus bringing the Vietnam Memorial into historical context." (as quoted by Leo Seligsohn in *Smithsonian*)

11. Probably not. The Vietnam War was fought against Asian peoples. The Chinese provided backing for our enemy in that war. So, it is unlikely Maya Lin would have been considered at all if the competition had not been anonymous.

Getting the Main Idea

Her work draws the viewers into it and allows them to express the emotions they are feeling. Thus, they leave the place feeling healed.

Applying What You've Learned

Answers will vary.

AN WANG

Remembering the Facts

1. It was a period of Chinese history in the 1920's and 1930's when warlords were struggling for power.
2. He began school in the third grade at age six; there was no kindergarten, first, or second grade in the school where his father taught.
3. His grandmother taught him the values of Confucius: (any two) moderation, patience, balance, and simplicity.
4. Electrical engineering
5. A Chinese government project involving the designing and building of transmitters and radios for government troops
6. The Chinese government sent a group of engineers to the United States to study American companies, then bring back their knowledge to help rebuild China.
7. The Communists had taken over.
8. His computer memory core invention
9. The desktop calculator
10. *(any two)* Bringing Chinese engineers to the United States to study; the Wang Center in Boston; an outpatient clinic at Massachusetts General Hospital; the Wang Institute; a computer plant in Boston's Chinatown

Understanding the Story

Answers will vary:

11. Wang overcame a great many problems at a young age. He lived through war, being separated from his family early in life, and the loss of both parents and a sister. Through all these problems, he was able to keep going and find success. By the time he arrived in the United States at the age of 25, he knew he would be able to survive. Since he had already lived through so much, he felt confident he could handle whatever came his way.

12. He was a king because he ran his huge company like a benevolent dictator. He was peaceful, because of his philosophy of life, which involved moderation, balance, patience, and simplicity.

Getting the Main Idea

Dr. Wang made an outstanding contribution to American life. His invention of the memory core made possible the modern computer. His many other inventions made life easier for millions of workers. Despite his great wealth, he chose to live simply—giving back much to his community.

Applying What You've Learned

Answers will vary.

HAING NGOR

Remembering the Facts

1. *The Killing Fields*
2. He was tutoring high school students to support himself; she was one of his pupils.
3. Phnom Penh, the capital of Cambodia
4. There were not enough doctors in Cambodia.
5. General Lon Nol

6. Phnom Penh fell to the Khmer Rouge.

7. *(any three)* They were executed; starvation; disease; unsanitary conditions; lack of medicine; long hours of labor.

8. He escaped to Thailand.

9. He used his fame to bring attention to what was happening in Cambodia.

10. He gave most of his money to help refugee children around the world.

Understanding the Story

Answers will vary:

11. Surviving under the rule of the Khmer Rouge required good acting every day. He had to pretend to be ignorant and uneducated. He had to hide the fact that he was a doctor. He had to learn to get food secretly and hide it. He learned to avoid the attention of the Khmer Rouge. He had to stand up to questioning, acting innocent even when his life was in jeopardy. The prize for success in this acting job was survival.

12. He, like most other residents of the capital city, did not really believe he was in danger. He thought that, as a doctor, he would be a valued person under any regime and so would escape harm. There was no way anyone could have imagined the horror that was to come.

Getting the Main Idea

Perseverance in the face of unbeatable odds; generosity in using his new-found fame and wealth to help others.

Applying What You've Learned

A variety of international relief agencies work to help people in trouble. An individual could donate money to one of these agencies. A person with medical skills could donate time working for one of these agencies. An individual could contact an agency and ask how else he or she could help (for example, collecting food or used clothing to be sent to the people in need).

Seiji Ozawa

Remembering the Facts

1. Because of Kaisaku Ozawa's pacifist activities
2. Kaisaku Ozawa was not allowed to practice dentistry in Japan.
3. Atomic bombs were dropped on Hiroshima and Nagasaki.
4. He had been led to believe that all Americans were monsters; instead they were "happy young people with chewing gum."
5. He broke both index fingers in a soccer game.
6. He earned his fare by working on a freighter.
7. Leonard Bernstein
8. Conductor of the Boston Symphony Orchestra
9. Seiji Ozawa Concert Hall
10. The fiftieth anniversary of the end of World War II

Understanding the Story

Answers will vary:

11. The Japanese in 1941 were already involved in World War II. They had been invading other Asian countries for some years before that. On December 7, 1941, they bombed Pearl Harbor. Pacifists were seen as working against the government.
12. His father's pacifist ideas were influential. But also, the war cast a shadow over his childhood. There were many air raids where he lived. His best friend was killed in the bombing. There was little food for the family. Traditional childhood activities were suspended.

Getting the Main Idea

Ozawa is a very influential musician in the United States. He is beloved as conductor of the Boston Symphony Orchestra. His music has brought much pleasure to millions. In addition, his special concerts for the fiftieth anniversary of the end of World War II have brought a message of peace and unity to music lovers everywhere.

Applying What You've Learned

Answers will vary:

Favorite hymns; classical music; or any type of music that gives a peaceful feeling.

KRISTI YAMAGUCHI

Remembering the Facts

1. Dorothy Hamill
2. She got up at 4:00 A.M.
3. She was Yamaguchi's singles coach for many years.
4. Rudi Galindo
5. Skaters must trace figures on the ice, first with one foot, then the other. They are judged on how well they trace. Compulsory figures were eliminated from competitions in 1990.
6. She was relaxed. There was less pressure on her to win first place.
7. They can no longer compete in amateur competitions like the Olympics. They can use their talent to earn money.
8. Because she was Japanese American
9. She performs with "Stars on Ice."

Understanding the Story

Answers will vary:

10. They would have less time to spend with friends. They would have to concentrate on one activity to the exclusion of others. They would have to spend an enormous amount of money on lessons, costumes, skates, etc. Going to school and practicing for hours would be a grueling combination.
11. Either: Natural talent is needed as a base from which to grow; but natural talent without hard work to develop it will not go far.

Getting the Main Idea

She is a person who had a goal in life and worked hard to achieve it. She remains modest in her success. She seems to keep things in perspective.

Applying What You've Learned

Answers will vary.

NORIYUKI "PAT" MORITA

Remembering the Facts

1. Spinal tuberculosis
2. A relocation camp in Arizona: Tulelake Internment Center
3. They were afraid some Japanese Americans might be loyal to Japan and attempt to sabotage the United States.
4. Morita's father died, and the family could not hold on to the restaurant.
5. He was restless. It wasn't really what he wanted to do for the rest of his life. He wanted to get into show business.
6. He wasn't handsome, and he couldn't sing or dance. But he was good at telling jokes.
7. Arnold, a hamburger shop owner
8. *Mr. T. and Tina*
9. It was his first serious role. It was the first time he had played a serious, full-dimensional Japanese character instead of a comic.
10. It shows a person who deals with problems with compassion, understanding, and knowledge instead of violence. It shows Miyagi as a father figure with solid values.

Understanding the Story

Answers will vary:

11.   There is a saying that "all is fair in love and war." The military did not feel that they could take any chances with the Japanese Americans who, for the most part, lived along the West Coast. There were fears of Japanese Americans collaborating with the enemy or sabotaging targets in the United States. If there was a Japanese invasion of the West Coast, the military feared that some Japanese Americans would work with their native countrymen instead of being loyal to the United States.

12.   About 110,000 Japanese Americans, most of whom were loyal citizens, were relocated. They had little notice, and often were forced to just walk away from their businesses and homes. Many of these people were locked up for four years. It would be impossible to make up for their mental suffering.

Getting the Main Idea

Cinderella went from rags to riches. From an early life of misfortune and sadness, Cinderella persevered and kept a kind and gentle outlook. She was rewarded when the prince fell in love with her, and her life was magically transformed. Morita too suffered much as a child. It was not until he was in his fifties that his life turned around.

Applying What You've Learned

Answers will vary:

Imagine waking up every day in an armed camp, surrounded by guards in a tower. You have done nothing to deserve this, except to be born Japanese American.

Yo-Yo Ma

Remembering the Facts

1. Both of his parents were gifted musicians.

2. He wanted to play something bigger than his sister's violin. So, he chose the cello.

3. He broke down longer pieces and taught him two measures a day. Then those two measures were added to what he had already learned. Ma practiced in short sessions of five to ten minutes a day. During that time, he was to concentrate intensely.

4. Juilliard School of Music

5. Chinese culture is very strict and structured. Children must be quiet and submissive. American culture is more permissive. Children are allowed to speak up and state their opinions.

6. He hoped to be able to bring the cultural threads of his life into perspective.

7. Avery Fisher Prize

8. He learned to get some balance in his life. He slowed down and gave fewer concerts per year.

9. It is a computer technique that makes one cello sound like 60.

10. It was the composer who had the vision to create the piece of music. Ma feels he is a vehicle for expressing the original intentions of the composer.

Understanding the Story

Answers will vary:

11. It would probably be most helpful for the person to talk about the problem with someone else who has dealt with it. By learning to analyze and understand things about each of the two cultures, the person can learn to put things in perspective.

12. It is always hard for a teenager to be different from the other kids. Being a child prodigy or being very talented in some

other way is a wonderful gift. But when the other kids tease or ostracize the gifted child, it is difficult to handle. This sort of situation usually works itself out with more maturity.

Getting the Main Idea

A musician must have two components to be truly gifted. Just playing all the right notes at the right time is not enough. To be meaningful, music must also have feeling. A true musician must convey emotions to an audience.

Applying What You've Learned

Answers will vary.

DAVID HO

Remembering the Facts

1. Taiwan

2. Harvard Medical School emphasized research.

3. He came in contact with two men suffering an unusual combination of symptoms. Soon, more cases of the unknown disease popped up. Dr. Ho could find nothing like this disease in the scientific literature. He was curious and began researching the disease.

4. The body's disease-fighting system

5. HIV attacks a kind of white blood cell called a helper T cell. These cells are the body's first line of defense against disease. When the cells are destroyed, the person is defenseless against other infections such as pneumonia. While the person may appear healthy for years, AIDS will appear and is always fatal.

6. The person tests HIV positive but appears to be healthy.

7. It means that HIV is not transmitted by casual contact such as a dirty drinking glass, coughs, sneezes, etc.

8. Aaron Diamond AIDS Research Center (the Diamond Center)

9. If a cure is not found, there will be more and more cases of AIDS. AIDS is very expensive to treat. So, it will be cheaper to put the money into research now (as well as alleviating much human suffering if a cure is found).

10. By diagnosing Magic Johnson with AIDS and by serving as his doctor

Understanding the Story

Answers will vary:

11. People were reading about others who had AIDS. But unless they knew someone who had the disease, it didn't really affect them. Magic Johnson was a very popular basketball player, beloved by fans for his skill on the basketball court as well as for his magnetic personality. Finding out that he had the fatal disease made it really hit home for millions of fans. Suddenly the disease became one that could strike anyone.

12. YES or NO. Possible answers include:

    YES: It is a terrifying disease that is spreading rapidly. It may take years to piece together the viral components needed to make an effective vaccine. Without funds, research cannot proceed.

    NO: It is getting enough money. There are other killer diseases (heart disease and cancer, for example) that need our funds, too.

Getting the Main Idea

Dr. David Ho and his researchers are trying to solve the puzzle of the HIV virus and AIDS. This is one of the worst epidemics in history, rapidly spreading and out of control. It is in everyone's best interest to find a cure or vaccine for this terrible disease as soon as possible.

Applying What You've Learned

Answers will vary.

Wendy Lee Gramm

Remembering the Facts

1. A company would pay the fare for a worker to come from another country. The worker would then be obligated to work for that company until the fare had been paid off.

2. There was a law against Asians marrying white Americans. If the men wanted to marry, they had to send back to their native land for a bride of their own race.

3. They worked in support of the South Korean war effort.

4. He was the first person of Asian descent to be promoted into management.

5. Americans were afraid that the Soviet Union was ahead in the space race. So, math and science were pushed hard in the schools to train more scientists. This influenced Gramm to study math.

6. Texas A & M

7. Phil Gramm won a seat in the U.S. House of Representatives.

8. Chairman of the Commodity Futures Trading Commission

9. It is a promise to buy or sell a commodity at a specific price on a certain date.

10. Bill Clinton became president. He was of a different political party and would appoint someone of his own party.

Understanding the Story

Answers will vary:

11. *Pros:* As wife of a famous politician, it would be easier for her to be noticed. People would know her name. Her husband could influence other senators to support her nomination.

    Cons: Many people would think she got the job because she was "someone's wife" rather than on her own merits. She would always be working to prove herself.

12. *Pros:* Many Americans see Asian Americans as the "model minority." They have an image as hardworking and good citizens. Since America in the next century will become more and

more of a melting pot, a mixed marriage may be very acceptable to most Americans.

Cons: Some people may be prejudiced against Asian Americans.

Getting the Main Idea

Gramm has been in a visible and responsible position for many years. She has proved herself to be versatile and effective as an administrator. Her success in the demanding field of economics is a plus for every Asian American.

Applying What You've Learned

Answers will vary.

ELLISON ONIZUKA

Remembering the Facts

1. They were field hands on a sugar plantation.
2. Eagle Scout
3. That was the season for harvesting coffee beans and the children were needed to work in the fields.
4. All astronauts had been white. The dream seemed impossible to reach.
5. Aerospace engineering
6. He went with them on flights and made sure new aircraft systems that were being tested were working correctly.
7. First Asian American (or Japanese American) in space, first Buddhist in space, and first Hawaiian in space
8. *(any two)* Kona coffee; macadamia nuts; Buddhist medallion from his father; patches from the Japanese-American 442nd Combat Team
9. A malfunctioning booster rocket
10. The Ellison S. Onizuka Space Center

Understanding the Story

Answers will vary:

11. Personality is important for success in any field. Astronauts must work in close quarters as a member of a team for extended periods of time. A person who could not get along with others would cause a lot of problems. Astronauts also have many occasions for speaking to groups of people and for giving interviews to newspapers, magazines, television, and radio. It is important for them to be able to relate well to other people and to project a confident and friendly manner.

12. The story of the Japanese American 442nd Combat Team is explained in more detail in the story on Daniel Inouye (pages 1–5). At first, no Asian Americans were accepted into the American fighting forces during World War II. Asian Americans worked hard to obtain the opportunity to prove their loyalty by fighting. The 442nd was formed of Japanese-American men, mainly from Hawaii. They became the most decorated army unit in World War II. Onizuka admired these men for their courage and loyalty to their country.

Getting the Main Idea

He worked hard to achieve his lifelong goal of becoming an astronaut. After achieving his dream, he spent much time sharing his wisdom with schoolchildren across the country.

Applying What You've Learned

Answers will vary.

CARLOS BULOSAN

Remembering the Facts

1. They mortgaged the farm to finance an education for one of their sons. Then they were unable to meet the payments.

2. His family could not escape their poverty, so he went out to make his own way.

3. He worked as a houseboy for an American woman.

4. He hoped it would offer him a better life.

5. Many Americans were out of work because of the Depression. Competition was stiff for the remaining jobs, and many resented the newly arrived immigrants who would compete for those jobs.

6. He was forced to go to Alaska to work in a fish cannery.

7. He tried to organize them into labor unions. Later, he realized he could have more impact as a writer.

8. *America Is in the Heart*

9. *(any one)* His years of struggle, abuse, and illness; his work to unite Filipinos in America; how his writing helped him reach his goals

10. A new generation of Asian Americans became interested in their roots and beginnings. *America Is in the Heart* was reprinted and has since become a fixture in Asian-American studies.

Understanding the Story

Answers will vary:

11. He was a voracious reader of all kinds of books. He used his time while recuperating from illness to read everything he could find.

12. America is more than a geographic location. It is a feeling that lives within people's hearts. It is democracy, freedom for all, and equality. It is the ideals upon which our country was founded.

Getting the Main Idea

America Is in the Heart is a detailed account of what life was like in the Philippines in the early 1900's. It makes it clear why so many people sought to come to America, where they hoped to find an easier life. *America Is in the Heart* goes on to chronicle the racism and despair immigrants faced when they arrived in America. Finally, it tells how one man was able to overcome these barriers to become a spokesperson for his people.

Applying What You've Learned

Answers will vary.

JOSE ARUEGO

Remembering What You've Learned

1. Manila, the Philippines
2. Law
3. He began practicing law and decided he didn't like it and wasn't good at it.
4. Comic books and animals
5. To study at the Parsons School of Design
6. Most of the cartoons he drew were rejected. He was paid only for the average 1 in 20 cartoons that were published.
7. He wrote and illustrated a book, *The King and His Friends.* While the book was not a best-seller, it brought his illustrations to the attention of book publishers.
8. Funny animals
9. That it be appealing to children
10. *(any one) Whose Mouse Are You?* and *Leo the Late Bloomer*

Understanding the Story

Answers will vary:

11. There was a lot of pressure on him to go to law school. His father, sister, and friends had done so.
12. Aruego is still growing as an artist. He is not stuck in a rut, using the same techniques over and over. He is willing to experiment with new ideas.

Getting the Main Idea

You will work at your career for many years. It is important to consider your aptitude for different kinds of work and choose something you have the ability to do well. You should also consider what types of activities make you happy. A person who loves to be outside might be miserable stuck in an office, for example.

Applying What You've Learned

Answers will vary. Choose a simple plot, then convey the story line in a series of pictures. The result will be like a comic strip. An actual picture book, such as those done by Aruego, will usually consist of 32 such pictures. In this exercise, use four to eight pictures. They can be simple stick figures or more complex drawings.

DUSTIN NGUYEN

Remembering the Facts

1. In 1954, the Geneva Convention divided the country into two parts at the 17th parallel.
2. North Vietnam was Communist; South Vietnam was Nationalist.
3. They were Communist soldiers who were experts in guerrilla warfare. They were trained by the North Vietnamese and backed by the Chinese.
4. President Lyndon B. Johnson
5. 1973
6. Nguyen's father had written anti-North Vietnamese propaganda. The Communists would have executed him when they took over Saigon.
7. The U.S. government had set up a refugee camp there.
8. Martial arts, especially Tae Kwon Do
9. *21 Jump Street*
10. DARE (Drug Abuse Resistance Education); antigang work

Understanding the Story

Answers will vary:

11. Many Americans had friends or loved ones killed or wounded in the war. The war had been the longest and most costly in America's history. It was also a war that we could not win. The Vietnam War had deeply divided America, leaving many people angry and bitter. Vietnamese refugees, although mostly innocent bystanders in the war, reminded people of all these things. Some people may have lumped all Vietnamese into one category and hated them all.

12. It would tend to put all other problems in perspective. Once you've barely escaped with your life and nothing else, you would know that whatever came along, you could deal with it.

Getting the Main Idea

He followed his heart and became an actor. Then, when he was successful in his field, he used his fame and influence to work for the betterment of other young Asian Americans.

Applying What You've Learned

Answers will vary:

Language barriers; strange customs; different climate; losing one's heritage.

Additional Activities

Daniel K. Inouye

1. During World War II, Japanese Americans on the West Coast were rounded up and placed in internment camps. Read more about this subject.

2. View a copy of the movie *Go for Broke!*

3. Find out more about the Watergate hearings.

4. Find out more about the Iran-Contra scandal.

5. Read Inouye's autobiography *Journey to Washington.* This book was written for Inouye's son, explaining the story of his life and the events that led up to Inoye's entering politics.

Maxine Hong Kingston

1. Read one or more of Kingston's books:
   - *The Woman Warrior: Memoirs of a Girlhood Among Ghosts*
   - *China Men*
   - *Tripmaster Monkey: His Fake Book*

2. Find out more about the building of the transcontinental railroad, especially the role of the Chinese in this monumental project.

3. Find out more about Chinatown in San Francisco.

4. Read about the role of the Chinese in the California Gold Rush.

I.M. Pei

1. Report on one of I.M. Pei's buildings. You may find pictures in books about American architecture. Some of his famous works are:

   • Mile High Center, Denver, Colorado

   • Place Ville-Marie, Montreal, Canada

   • Kips Bay Plaza apartments, New York City

   • Society Hill Towers, Philadelphia, Pennsylvania

   • Henry R. Luce Foundation Chapel, Taiwan

   • National Center for Atmospheric Research, Boulder, Colorado

   • Everson Museum of Art, Syracuse, New York

   • Herbert F. Johnson Museum of Art, Cornell University, Ithaca, New York

   • Terminal for John F. Kennedy International Airport, New York City

   • John Hancock Building, Boston, Massachusetts

   • East Building annex to the National Gallery of Art in Washington, D.C.

   • Government Center, Boston, Massachusetts

   • John F. Kennedy Library, Boston, Massachusetts

   • Fragrant Hill Hotel, Beijing, China

   • Weisner Building, MIT, Cambridge, Massachusetts

   • Bank of China, Hong Kong

   • Meyerson Symphony Center, Dallas, Texas

   • Louvre addition, Paris, France

   • Rock 'n' Roll Hall of Fame, Cleveland, Ohio

2. Read about the two designers with whom Pei studied at Harvard: Walter Gropius and Marcel Breuer. They founded the Bauhaus, a school of art and modern design.

3. Find out more about the Communist revolution in China.

Maya Lin

1. Find pictures of Maya Lin's major works:
   - Vietnam Veterans Memorial, Washington, D.C.
   - Civil Rights Memorial, Montgomery, Alabama
   - Museum of African Art, New York City
   - *The Women's Table*, Yale University
   - *Groundswell*, Ohio State University
   - Clock in Pennsylvania Station, New York City
2. Find out more about the controversy that sprang up regarding the Vietnam Veterans Memorial.
3. Find a picture of Frederick Hart's statue that was installed about 120 feet from the entrance to Lin's Memorial. Compare the two works. Which do you find more satisfying as a memorial?
4. Find out more about the Vietnam War.

An Wang

1. Find out more about Wang Laboratories. Who runs it now? What are some of the company's products?
2. Read more about the Age of Confusion in Chinese history.
3. Read about the sayings of Confucius, the famous Chinese philosopher.
4. Find out about the first computers. What did they look like? How did they work?
5. Read the autobiography of An Wang: *Lessons*.

Haing Ngor

1. Obtain a map of Southeast Asia. Locate the countries of Cambodia, Vietnam, Laos, and Thailand.
2. Read about the secret bombing of Cambodia by the U.S. Air Force that went on for 14 months in 1969 and 1970. The bombings shocked the nation when they were revealed in 1973, because while they were ongoing, American officials—

including President Richard Nixon—avowed that Cambodian neutrality was being respected.

3. Read about the invasion of Cambodia in May 1970 by American troops.

4. On April 29, 1970, President Nixon announced that American troops would invade Cambodia. News of the invasion sparked rioting on college campuses across the nation. Four students were killed and many more wounded by National Guardsmen at Kent State University in Ohio. Two students were shot and killed at Jackson State College in Jackson, Mississippi, by highway patrolmen. Read more about these turbulent times on our nation's campuses.

5. View a copy of the movie *The Killing Fields.*

6. Read Haing Ngor's autobiography *A Cambodian Odyssey.*

7. Find out about the political situation in Cambodia today.

Seiji Ozawa

1. Find out more about the dropping of the atomic bombs on Hiroshima and Nagasaki.

2. One piece of music Ozawa chose to mark the fiftieth anniversary of the end of World War II was Gustav Mahler's *Symphony No. 2,* "Resurrection." Obtain a recording of this symphony and listen to it.

Kristi Yamaguchi

1. Read about Dorothy Hamill, Kristi Yamaguchi's inspiration.

2. Find out more about the internment of Japanese Americans during World War II.

3. Watch a figure-skating program on television.

4. Read about other famous women skaters, such as Sonja Henie, Carol Heiss, or Peggy Fleming.

5. Take a walk down the cereal aisle in a grocery store. Make a list of cereals that have athletes on the box, endorsing the product.

Noriyuki "Pat" Morita

1. Read more about the Japanese-American relocation during World War II.

2. If you haven't seen them, watch one of the *Karate Kid* series: *The Karate Kid, Karate Kid Part II, Karate Kid Part III,* or *The Next Karate Kid.*

Yo-Yo Ma

1. Yo-Yo Ma has made over 50 recordings. Check one out at your local library. Listen to it and see why Ma is acclaimed the world over.

2. Another child prodigy in music is Sarah Chang. She is a violinist born to Korean-American parents. Born in 1981, Chang played with the New York Philharmonic Orchestra when she was only eight years old. Find out more about her.

3. Another famous cellist is Pablo Casals. Find out more about him.

David Ho

1. Read about the latest developments in the fight against AIDS.

2. Find out about the work of the Diamond Center in New York.

3. Read about how the immune system fights disease.

Wendy Lee Gramm

1. Find out about how futures contracts and futures options work.

2. Read about the work of the Commodity Futures Trading Commission.

3. Read about the Korean War, 1950–1952.

4. Find out about the space race between the United States and the Soviet Union.

5. Read about the impact on American education of the launching of *Sputnik.*

Ellison Onizuka

1. Read Daniel and Susan Cohen's book, *Heroes of the* Challenger, for more about the *Challenger* astronauts.
2. Find out about the Kona coffee fields in Hawaii.
3. Write for information about the Ellison S. Onizuka Space Center Museum in Kona, Hawaii.
4. Find out more about the space shuttle program.
5. Read about the history of the U.S. space program.

Carlos Bulosan

1. Read *America Is in the Heart* or another of Bulosan's works.
2. Find out more about the Great Depression of the 1930's.
3. Find out about the role of Filipino soldiers in World War II.
4. Read about the World War II battles that took place in the Pacific Islands.

Jose Aruego

1. Jose Aruego has written and/or illustrated many books. Use the card catalog at your local public library to locate some of his books. Write a paragraph telling about one of them.
2. Draw a cartoon on a subject of local interest that could be used in your school or town newspaper. Make your cartoon funny, but also have it convey a message about an issue.

Dustin Nguyen

1. Read more about the story of the Vietnam War, including the fall of Saigon in 1975.
2. Find out more about DARE (Drug Abuse Resistance Education).

References

Daniel K. Inouye

"Daniel K. Inouye." *Current Biography Yearbook,* 1987, pp. 268–272.

Goodsell, Jane. *Daniel Inouye.* New York: Thomas Y. Crowell, 1977.

Inouye, Daniel K. *Journey to Washington.* Englewood Cliffs, NJ: Prentice-Hall, 1967.

Morey, Janet Nomura, and Dunn, Wendy. *Famous Asian Americans.* New York: Cobblehill Books, 1992.

Maxine Hong Kingston

Kingston, Maxine Hong. *China Men.* New York: Alfred A. Knopf, 1980.

———. *Tripmaster Monkey: His Fake Book.* New York: Alfred A. Knopf, 1989.

———. *The Woman Warrior: Memoirs of a Girlhood Among Ghosts.* New York: Alfred A. Knopf, 1976.

"Maxine Hong Kingston." *Contemporary Authors,* Vol. 38. Detroit: Gale Research, 1993, pp. 206–210.

"Maxine Hong Kingston." *Current Biography Yearbook,* 1990, pp. 359–363.

Morey, Janet Nomura, and Dunn Wendy. *Famous Asian Americans.* New York: Cobblehill Books, 1992.

I.M. Pei

Ergas, G. Aimee. *Artists from Michelangelo to Maya Lin,* Vol. 2. New York: Gale Research, 1995, pp. 336–341.

"I.M. Pei." *Current Biography Yearbook,* 1990, pp. 495–499.

Who's Who in American Art, 1984, p. 714.

Maya Lin

Daley, William. *The Chinese Americans.* New York: Chelsea House Publishers, 1987, p. 79.

Ergas, G. Aimee. *Artists from Michelangelo to Maya Lin.* New York: Gale Research, 1995, pp. 265–271.

"Maya Lin." *Current Biography Yearbook,* 1993, pp. 349–353.

Zinsser, W.K. "I realized her tears were becoming part of the memorial." *Smithsonian,* September, 1991, pp. 32–40.

An Wang

"An Wang." *American Men and Women of Science,* Vol. VII, 1982, p. 407.

"An Wang." *Current Biography Yearbook,* 1987, pp. 586–590.

Wang, An, with Linden, Eugene. *Lessons: An Autobiography.* Reading, MA: Addison-Wesley, 1986.

Haing Ngor

Bailey, Thomas A., and Kennedy, David M. *The American Pageant.* Lexington, MA: D.C. Heath, 1983.

Ngor, Haing, with Warner, Roger. *A Cambodian Odyssey.* New York: Macmillan, 1987.

Wood, Daniel B. "His Life Is Cambodia's Story." *The Christian Science Monitor,* March 31, 1988.

Seiji Ozawa

Bisbee, Dana. "Childhood Inspiration." *Boston Herald,* October 17, 1994.

Dyer, Richard. "Ozawa keys season to WWII anniversary." *The Boston Globe,* September 30, 1994.

Pfeiffer, Ellen. "Inaugural Day of Seiji Ozawa Concert Hall at Tanglewood." *Boston Herald,* July 8, 1994.

Pincus, Andrew L. "Ozawa, the bomb, and Tanglewood." *Berkshire Eagle* (Pittsfield, MA), February 24, 1995.

"Seiji Ozawa." *Current Biography Yearbook,* 1968, pp. 298–300.

Kristi Yamaguchi

"Kristi Yamaguchi." *Current Biography Yearbook,* 1992, pp. 616–619.

"Kristi Yamaguchi." *Notable Asian Americans.* Helen Zia and Susan B. Gall, eds. New York: Gale Research, 1995, pp. 423–425.

Swift, E.M. "All That Glitters." *Sports Illustrated,* Vol. 77, Issue 25, December 14, 1992, pp. 70–80.

Noriyuki "Pat" Morita

Davis, Chuck. "Noriyuki 'Pat' Morita Full of Life Now—Not Bitter." *Daily Oklahoman*, June 30, 1989.

Haithman, Daine. "Morita Uses Timing in 'Karate Kid' Role." *Dallas Morning News*, July 5, 1986.

Jones, Gwen. "My life has been a series of Cinderella stories." *Los Angeles Herald Examiner,* March 25, 1985.

"Noriyuki 'Pat' Morita." *Notable Asian Americans.* Helen Zia and Susan B. Gall, Eds. New York: Gale Research, 1995, pp. 266–267.

Stark, John. "After a Lifetime of Misfortune, *Karate Kid*'s Noriyuki 'Pat' Morita Battles His Way to a Happy Ending." *People* magazine, June 30, 1986, pp. 101–103.

Wuntch, Philip. "Script of a Lifetime." *Dallas Morning News*, July 1, 1989.

Yo-Yo Ma

Blum, David. "Profiles: A Process Larger Than Oneself." *New Yorker*, May 1, 1989, pp. 41+.

"The Courage to Go Forth: Yo-Yo Ma in Conversation." *Economist*, Vol. 322, no. 7746, February 15, 1992, p. 107.

"1992 Artists of the Year." *Musical America,* Vol. 112, Issue 1, January, 1992, pp. 14–15.

"Yo-Yo Ma." *Current Biography Yearbook,* 1982, pp. 254–257.

"Yo-Yo Ma." *Notable Asian Americans.* Helen Zia and Susan B. Gall, Eds. New York: Gale Research, 1995, pp. 227–230.

David Ho

Cerio, Gregory. "Forward Ho." *New York* magazine, March 16, 1992, p. 36.

"David Ho." *Notable Asian Americans.* Helen Zia and Susan B. Gall, Eds. New York: Gale Research, 1995, pp. 113–114.

"David Ho." *Who's Who among Asian Americans 1994/95.* Amy L. Unterburger, Ed. Detroit: Gale Research, Inc., p. 200.

Woodard, Catherine. "Unraveling AIDS: City Lab and Its Director Work at the Cutting Edge." *New York Newsday,* September 7, 1993.

Wendy Lee Gramm

Bradley, Jennifer. "Hillary's Nightmare." *The New Republic,* April 3, 1995.

Gramm, Wendy L. "The Economy, A Women's Issue." *The Wall Street Journal,* March 22, 1994, p. A14.

Morey, Janet, and Dunn, Wendy. *Famous Asian Americans.* New York: Cobblehill Books, 1992, pp. 44–57.

"Wendy Lee Gramm." *Notable Asian Americans.* Helen Zia and Susan B. Gall, Eds. New York: Gale Research, 1995, pp. 92–93.

Ellison Onizuka

Cohen, Daniel, and Cohen, Susan. *Heroes of the* Challenger. New York: Pocket Books, 1986.

"Ellison Onizuka." *The Golden Library of North American Biographies*, Vol. 4, Danbury, CT: Grolier & Co., 1994, pp. 179–180.

"Ellison Onizuka: 1946-1986." *Time*, February 10, 1986.

"Ellison Onizuka." *Notable Asian Americans.* Helen Zia and Susan B. Gall, Eds. New York: Gale Research, 1995, pp. 302–304.

Kitano, Harry. *The Japanese Americans.* New York: Chelsea House Publishers, 1987, p. 88.

Morey, Janet, and Dunn, Wendy. *Famous Asian Americans.* New York: Cobblehill Books, 1992, pp. 115–127.

Yoshihashi, Pauline. "Three Boys' Dreams of Space, Three Deaths in the Sky." *The New York Times*, February 11, 1986.

Carlos Bulosan

Bulosan, Carlos. *America Is in the Heart.* New York: Harcourt, Brace and Co., 1943.

"Carlos Bulosan," *Notable Asian Americans,* Helen Zia and Susan B. Gall, Eds, New York: Gale Research, 1995, pp. 20–22.

"Carlos Bulosan," *Current Biography Yearbook,* 1946, pp. 82–83.

Jose Aruego

"Jose Aruego." *Children's Literature Review,* Vol. 5. Detroit: Gale Research, 1983, pp. 27-32.

"Jose Aruego." *Contemporary Authors,* Vol. 42, pp. 21–23.

"Jose Aruego." *Fourth Book of Junior Authors and Illustrators.* H.W. Wilson, 1978, p. 15.

"Jose Aruego" (biographical profile), Greenwillow Books, 1986.

"Jose Aruego." *Something About the Author,* Vol. 68. Detroit: Gale Research, 1992, pp. 15–18.

Dustin Nguyen

Marvis, Barbara. *Contemporary American Success Stories: Famous People of Asian Ancestry,* Vol. 4. M. Lane Publications, 1994.

Morey, Janet, and Dunn, Wendy. *Famous Asian Americans.* New York: Cobblehill Books, 1992, pp. 103–114.

Vespa, Mary, with Alexander, Michael. "A Survivor of the Fall of Saigon, *21 Jump Street*'s Dustin Nguyen Relives the Ordeal on TV." *People* magazine, April 25, 1988.